古韵临平
时尚江南

Ancient Linping, Modern Jiangnan

王晓林 / 绘　　刘冰婕 / 文

ZHEJIANG UNIVERSITY PRESS
浙江大学出版社
·杭州·

天堂门户的河畔生活

临平拥有七千年人类繁衍史、五千年人类文明史、一千八百年文献记载史，以及一千年置官建城史。这片 286 平方千米的土地，是杭州北接上海、嘉兴、湖州的门户，处在杭嘉湖平原和长三角的圆心。

临平区诞生于 2021 年 4 月 9 日。彼时杭州市进行行政区划优化调整，将原余杭区以京杭大运河为界，分设为运河以西的新余杭区和运河以东的临平区。2000 多年来，大运河从位于杭州的运河南端北上并在临平境内东出，虽河道的变迁堪称沧海桑田，对临平的环抱之势始终不变，滋养出这片土地独有的运河风情。

所以，临平人文荟萃，底蕴深深。作为新区成立后出版的第一本绘本，我们谨记选题讨论时关于"可读性""接地气""烟火气"的定位，挂一漏万地选择了一些临平人认为很"临平"、外地人随手一翻就能感知的内容放到书里。

临平有临平人引以为傲的史前文明。茅山遗址出土面积达 5000 多平方米的水稻田，将临平境内的人类活动溯源到新石器时代；玉架山遗址 6 条环壕以及居住地、广场、墓地等遗迹，是目前唯一贯通马家浜文化、良渚文化、崧泽文化和钱山漾文化的遗址，是东南亚稻作文明体系最完整、最成熟的地区，也是史前江南、史前大运河的萌发地与展示地。

临平有本地人津津乐道的临平历史。临平在东汉时已因"临平湖"名载史册，晋时形成集市，隋唐以来是上塘河水路东出杭州的必经之地和第一大埠。临平镇建于北宋端拱元年（988），这也被认为是临平建城的开端。

临平有襟山带湖的自然地标——临平山与临平湖。临平山作为天目山最东端的余脉，景色荫翳而气质隐逸；临平湖作为时尚产业与休闲文化的汇聚地，从容娴静而又生机勃勃。

临平有最重要的运河文脉。大运河临平段由京杭大运河临平段和古上塘河组成。2013 年，大运河临平段（含两条河道、广济桥、桂芳桥）被列为全国重点文物保护单位。大运河的流经，让临平在"舟行天下"的年代成为一个连通江河湖海的交通资源高地，并由此带来繁荣的商业气息与活跃的文化交流。今天在临平的运河故道边，你能感受到人们对市井趣味的致敬与传承，这恰是运河文脉的活态注脚。

临平还有被科创与文创激活的乡野。城市化的激流滚滚而来，人群越来越聚集，田头的庄稼越来越孤单；大运河畔的乡野，却激荡着携手共富的矢志不移。我们在这里见到的村庄，变得既熟悉又年轻；道路、河流、塘里的作物、房屋和院子，经过一轮接着一轮的改头换面，正在成为一个个美丽乡村的样板、一个个共同富裕的代表。

我们希望用略高于生活的方式来表达临平，比如有趣的建筑、缤纷的植被、充满人文关怀的生活，以及尚未落成的精心规划。很遗憾没有办法展示临平的更多侧面，比如临光面店几十年来抚慰人心的早餐，菜市场美食的烟火缭绕，老绸厂改建的新天地文创园，旺旺、华味亨、新希望等零食工厂的快乐"剁手"游……不如，您亲自来吧，身"临"其境，我们"平"水相逢！

Embracing the Canal Bank Life
at the Gateway of Heaven

7,000 years ago, people began to live and reproduce in Linping. This place boasts 5,000 years of civilization with 1,800 years of documentary history and 1,000 years of official governance and city development. Spanning 286 square kilometers, it serves as a gateway to connect Hangzhou northwards to Shanghai, Jiaxing and Huzhou and also a center in Hangzhou—Jiaxing—Huzhou Plain and Yangtze River Delta.

On April 9, 2021, Linping District came into existence as a result of administrative division adjustments carried out by Hangzhou. The original Yuhang District was divided, creating a new Yuhang District to the west of the Canal and Linping District to the east. For over two thousand years, the Grand Canal has flowed north from the southern end of the Canal in Hangzhou and wandered eastward through the land of Linping. While the course of the river may have undergone drastic changes as time passes by, its enduring embrace of Linping has remained constant, nurturing the distinctive canal style that characterizes this region.

Therefore, Linping is a place of talents gathering and profound history. As the first picture book published following the establishment of the new district, we have considered the themes of "readability," "practicality," and "vibrancy" throughout our topic discussions. We have carefully selected the contents that reflect the essence of "Linping" as perceived by its residents, while also ensuring that outsiders can easily read with the book's contents.

Linping has a prehistoric civilization which local people are proud of. The archaeological discoveries at the Maoshan site provide evidence of early human activities in Linping, tracing back to the Neolithic Age through an expansive rice fields spanning over 5,000 square meters. With 6 ring trenches, residence, square, cemetery and other remains, Yujiashan is currently the only site which reflects the characteristics of the Majiabang culture, Liangzhu culture, Songze culture and Qianshanyang culture. It embodies the most complete and mature Southeast Asia rice civilization, and is also the birthplace and demonstration of prehistoric Jiangnan and Grand Canal culture.

Linping has a history that natives would talk about in enthusiasm. The name of Linping was found in the annals of time thanks to the fabled "Linping Lake" during the Eastern Han Dynasty. A bustling marketplace emerged during the Jin Dynasty. Since the Sui and Tang Dynasties, Linping has stood as the grandest port for the Shangtang River waterway flows eastward to Hangzhou. With its founding in the inaugural year (988) of Duangong during the Northern Song Dynasty, the evolution of Linping Town officially began.

Linping has natural landmarks agianst hills and by water such as Linping Mountain and Linping Lake. Linping Mountain, the easternmost vestige of the Tianmu Mountain range, unveils a sylvan landscape with tranquil beauty and seclusion. Meanwhile, Linping Lake serves as a nexus for the fashion industry and leisure culture, exuding a serene and vibrant ambiance.

Linping has the most important cultural legacy of the Great Canal. The Grand Canal (Linping section) is composed of the Beijing—Hangzhou Grand Canal (Linping section) and the Ancient Shangtang River. In 2013, the Linping section of the Grand Canal (including two river channels as well as the Guangji Bridge and the Guifang Bridge) was listed as key cultural relics sites under the protection of the state. Through the coursing waters of the Grand Canal, Linping flourished as a hub connecting rivers, lakes, and seas during the era when a boat is a major transportation tool. This in turn fostered a vibrant commerce and a dynamic culture. Today, strolling along the ancient canal road in Linping, we can still sense a living testament to the enduring spirit of the canal's legacy.

Linping also has the countryside vitalized by the science innovation as well as culture and creative industries. As the tide of urbanization surges forth, people gather together, leaving fields in solitude. However, in Linping's countryside along the

Grand Canal, people embark on a journey toward common prosperity with resolution. The villages that unfold before our eyes show a sense of familiarity and youthful vitality. The roads, rivers, and crops in the ponds, as well as the houses and yards, stand all as exquisite embodiment of village splendor. Each element acts as a testament to the rural beauty and common prosperity.

We hope to capture the essence of Linping in a manner that transcends the ordinary, through the interesting architecture, vibrant foliage, a lifestyle full of humanistic care, and also more plannings that are still awaiting its full realization. It is regrettable that we are unable to show all the details of Linping, such as the breakfast at Linguang Noodle Shop comforting people for decades, the delicious food at the vegetable market, the re-imagined Xintiandi Cultural Park, once an old silk factory, or many snack factories in Linping attracting hands-chopping people. Why not come here to experience yourself firsthand? Let's meet in Linping.

临平全景
Panorama of Linping

目录 *Contents*

临平夜景
Night View of Linping

PORTRAIT OF LINPING

临平画像

临平，杭州东北的门户，长江三角洲的圆心。

Linping is the gateway to northeast Hangzhou and the center of the Yangtze River Delta.

区域面积：286 平方千米

2022 年末常住人口：110.8 万人

下辖街道：运河街道、乔司街道、塘栖镇、崇贤街道、
临平街道、东湖街道、南苑街道、星桥街道

Area: 286 square kilometers

Permanent residents(at the end of 2022): 1,108,000

Subdistricts under its jurisdiction:
Yunhe Subdistrict, Qiaosi Subdistrict, Tangxi Town, Chongxian Subdistrict,
Linping Subdistrict, Donghu Subdistrict, Nanyuan Subdistrict and Xingqiao Subdistrict

作为浙江省首个快速路环线贯通的区县，临平境内拥有约 20 千米快速路环线，另有沪杭、杭浦、申嘉湖杭、杭州绕城等 4 条高速穿城而过，两条地铁、沪杭高铁让临平稳稳地"接沪融杭"。因此，一个临平人，可以通过地铁或者高架当天往返杭州各区，或者走高速往返湖州、嘉兴、宁波、义乌，还可以乘高铁当天往返上海、南京。发达的交通网，把临平人的圈子延伸到更高的山、更阔的海、更多元的生活方式。

As the first district in Zhejiang Province to be interconnected by expressway loop lines, Linping boasts an approximately 20-kilometer road network within its border. Furthermore, four major expressways traverse the city, including the Shanghai－Hang-zhou Expressway, Hangzhou－Pudong Expressway, Shanghai－Jiaxing－Huzhou－Hangzhou Expressway, and Ring Expressway of Hangzhou. The two subway lines and the Shanghai－Hangzhou High-speed Railway ensure convenient and reliable transportation links between Linping, Shanghai, and the other districts of Hangzhou. Consequently, residents of Linping can easily commute to any part of Hangzhou within a day via subway or viaduct, access neighboring cities such as Huzhou, Jiaxing, Ningbo, and Yiwu through expressways, and even travel to and from Shanghai and Nanjing via high-speed railways in the same day. This well-developed transportation network expands the horizons of Linping's residents, granting them access to higher mountains, broader seas, and a more diverse range of lifestyles.

交通发达，是临平自古以来的特点。

京杭大运河环抱临平而过，在境内延绵数十公里，其中最早的上塘河段，在秦始皇年代就已开通，此后一直承担从东部进出杭州的重要交通功能，南宋所设班荆馆（相当于现在的国宾馆）、宋高宗恭迎南归皇太后的驿站都位于上塘河畔。

到了元末，狭窄的上塘河常常干涸，于是开挖新河道，有了下塘河，也就是今天我们所说的京杭大运河塘栖段，塘栖自此成为运河重镇，粮食等水运大宗物资无比丰富。

今天，再发达的陆运仍然无法媲美水运的低成本。为直接沟通大运河与钱塘江，临平正从北端的博陆码头一路向南挖通运河二通道，为临平的运河发展添上新时代的笔墨。

Linping has long been renowned for its well-established transportation system back to ancient times.

The Beijing–Hangzhou Grand Canal encircles Linping, extending for dozens of kilometers. Among its sections, the earliest segment known as the Shangtang River was established during the Qin Dynasty (BC221–BC207). Since then, it has served as a crucial transportation route for entering and departing Hangzhou from the east. Notably, significant historical sites such as the Banjing Guan (comparable to the present-day state guesthouse) established during the Southern Song Dynasty and the post stations where Emperor Gaozong of the Song Dynasty welcomed the Empress Dowager upon her return are situated along the banks of the Shangtang River.

During the later years of the Yuan Dynasty, the narrow Shangtang River would frequently experience drying up. To address this issue, a new channel was excavated, which became the Xiatang River. Presently known as the Hangzhou–Tangxi section of the Beijing–Hangzhou Grand Canal, Tangxi has evolved into a significant canal town, boasting an abundant supply of food and other materials for water transportation.

Despite the advancements in land transportation, it still cannot compete with the lower cost of water transportation. Hence, Linping is undertaking the construction of a second canal channel that directly connects the Beijing–Hangzhou Grand Canal and the Qiantang River. This new channel will extend from the Bolu Wharf at the northern end of Linping to the southern region, ushering in a new era of canal development of the area.

京杭大运河
Beijing–Hangzhou Grand Canal

浙江理工大学（临平校区）
Zhejiang Sci-Tech University (Linping Campus)

大运河1986文创园
Grand Canal 1986 Creative Park

塘栖古镇
Tangxi Ancient Town

运河街道
Yunhe Subdistrict

运溪路
Yunxi Road

东湖高架
Donghu Elevated Expressway

运河二通道
The Second Canal Channel

塘栖镇
Tangxi Town

望梅高架
Wangmei Elevated Expressway

玉架山考古遗址公园
Yujia Mountain Archaeological Site Park

东湖街道
Donghu Subdistric

丁山湖
Dingshan Lake

超山风景区
Chaoshan Mountain Scenic Area

临平街道
Linping Subdistrict

地铁9号线
Metro Line 9

练杭高速 (S13)
Lianshi–Hangzhou Expressway

秋石北路
North Qiushi Road

秋石高架
Qiushi Elevated Expressway

临平公园（临平山）
Linping Park (Linping Mountain)

临平体育中心
Linping Sports Center

中国江南水乡博物馆
China Museum of Southern Water Town Culture

星桥街道
Xingqiao Subdistrict

疏港大道
Shugang Avenue

崇贤街道
Chongxian Subdistrict

杭州绕城高速
Ring Expressway of Hangzhou (G2501)

杭州跑步中心
Hangzhou Running Center

艺尚小镇
E-fashion Town

东湖公园
Donghu Park

沪杭甬高速 (S2)
Shanghai–Hangzhou–Ningbo Expressway

天都公园
Tiandu Park

留石高架
Liushi Elevated Expressway

临平南站
Linping South Railway Station

南苑街道
Nanyuan Subdistrict

杭浦高速 (S16)
Hangzhou–Pudong Expressway

地铁3号线
Metro Line 3

乔司街道
Qiaosi Subdistrict

沪杭高铁
Shanghai–Hangzhou High-speed Railway

高速公路 Expressway
快速路 Elevated Expressway
高铁 High-speed Railway
地铁 Metro
高速出入口 Expressway Exit and Entrance

临平的历史深度，不止运河两千年。

玉架山遗址出土的精美玉器是约 5000 年前良渚文化的经典器物，茅山遗址则贡献了国内考古发掘出土最长、最完整的史前独木舟。

三国时期古籍中就有关于"临平湖"的记载，其中有句"此湖塞，天下乱；此湖开，天下平"的政治寓言，被司马光收录进《资治通鉴》。

超山的梅园，珍藏着唐、宋的古梅树，承载着晚清民国金石大师吴昌硕对梅花的情有独钟、痴心不改。

临平东南，横亘着八千米原汁原味的钱塘江古海塘，记录着"人间天堂"杭州在清代作为御潮前线，筑城捍海的另一种艰辛故事……

临平的来路，被完整地收藏进中国江南水乡文化博物馆。这座建在临平、以地理文化为主题的博物馆恰如其名，不止于临平，而是着眼整个江南鱼米之乡，解开长三角何以发达富庶的密码。

The historical significance of Linping extends far beyond the 2000-year-old canal.

The Yujia Mountain site in Linping has uncovered remarkable discoveries of finely crafted jade artifacts, showcasing the exquisite craftsmanship of the Liangzhu culture dating back to 5,000 years. In addition, the Maoshan site in Linping has provided archaeologists with the longest and most complete prehistoric canoe found in China.

The "Linping Lake" can be found in the historical records of the Three Kingdoms. These texts include a political fable stating that when the lake is blocked, chaos ensues, but when it is unblocked, peace prevails. This fable was documented in *Zizhi Tongjian* (Comprehensive Mirror for Aid in Government) written by Sima Guang, a comprehensive historical text that chronicles the history of China.

The plum garden nestled in the Chaoshan Mountain is home to the precious ancient plum trees from the Tang and Song Dynasties. These trees hold a special place in the heart of Wu Changshuo, a renowned seal carver from the late Qing Dynasty and the Republic of China.

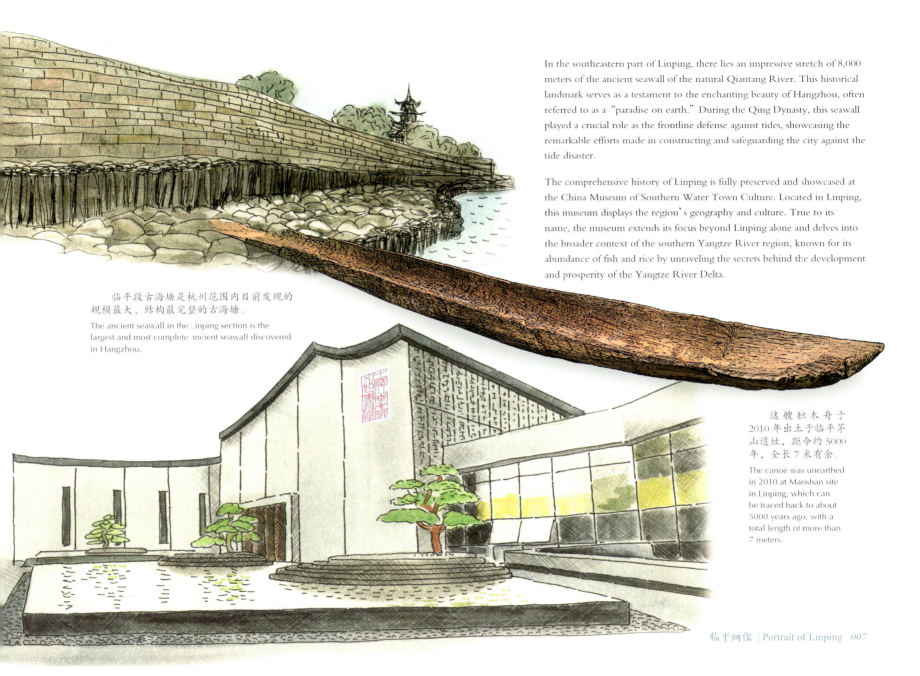

In the southeastern part of Linping, there lies an impressive stretch of 8,000 meters of the ancient seawall of the natural Qiantang River. This historical landmark serves as a testament to the enchanting beauty of Hangzhou, often referred to as a "paradise on earth." During the Qing Dynasty, this seawall played a crucial role as the frontline defense against tides, showcasing the remarkable efforts made in constructing and safeguarding the city against the tide disaster.

The comprehensive history of Linping is fully preserved and showcased at the China Museum of Southern Water Town Culture. Located in Linping, this museum displays the region's geography and culture. True to its name, the museum extends its focus beyond Linping alone and delves into the broader context of the southern Yangtze River region, known for its abundance of fish and rice by unraveling the secrets behind the development and prosperity of the Yangtze River Delta.

临平段古海塘是杭州范围内目前发现的规模最大、结构最完整的古海塘。
The ancient seawall in the Linping section is the largest and most complete ancient seawall discovered in Hangzhou.

这艘独木舟于 2010 年出土于临平茅山遗址，距今约 5000 年，全长 7 米有余。
The canoe was unearthed in 2010 at Maoshan site in Linping, which can be traced back to about 5000 years ago, with a total length of more than 7 meters.

LANDSCAPE OF MOUNTAI
ND LAKE ENJOYING
ATURAL-BORN PROSPERI

湖光山色自繁华

在长达 60 年的时间里，原临平镇一直是当地行政中心所在地，产业起步早、生活设施完备，有足够产业支撑的多层次消费商圈、充足的教育与医疗资源、已然成形并不断延伸的三维立体交通网络，加上并不太高的房价，这些构成了临平宜居宜业的底层逻辑。

In over past 60 years, as the site where the administrative center was located, the former Linping Town started early in industrial development and enjoyed fully-equipped facilities. The multilevel business circles of adequate industrial support, sufficient educational and medical resources, a well developed and constantly expanding 3D transport network, and local modest house prices all lay foundation for Linping as an ideal place to both live and work.

自古就有一山一湖以"临平"为名，山在西北，湖在东南。

临平山由北宋诗僧道潜记录过："五月临平山下路，藕花无数满汀洲。"光是山下美怎么够？当代人以临平山为载体建起了公园，给自己找了众乐乐之处。临平公园收藏了无数"80后""90后"的童年欢乐。携手登山的情侣、推车"遛娃"的家长、约会的中老年同学、跳广场舞的大妈，在公园里和谐相处，悠然自得。公园一直在不断修缮更新，2023年又迎来杜鹃园和环山步道的开放。

我有幸在春天踏足临平山。有年份的遮天乔木仿佛搭建起临平山的结界，一进入便感到清凉静心。光从林间洒下，因丁达尔效应而显得神圣静谧，山路上透着绿野仙踪的气息。恰逢杜鹃花期，一簇簇各色杜鹃填满了山体坡地的空隙。花儿完全无视游人，在穿透树叶的日光下兀自开着，成片成片地灿烂。"绝怜人境无车马，信有山林在市城。"临平公园算是把这样的美学发挥到极致了。

公园里时不时出现古人的题诗典故，读下来发现"隐逸"二字才是临平山最本真的文化内涵。我奔东来阁而去，一路上坡行至高处，一座金属榫卯结构的唐风塔阁高高伫立，古典又现代，应着东坡先生那句"谁似临平山上塔，亭亭，迎客西来送客行"。拾级而上，再由电梯登顶，只为一睹鳞次栉比的城郭尘寰。站在阁顶，四月的风送来一丝意外的清凉，几声鸟语来自某个缥缈的深处，俯视的开阔与超脱的畅快一起袭来。

In ancient times, there was a mountain and a lake named after "Linping," with the mountain in the northwest and the lake in the southeast.

As recorded by Daoqian, a monk and poet in the Northern Song Dynasty, "Walking along the foot of the Linping Mountain in the fifth lunar month, one will be captivated by numerous lotus flowers blooming on the water." It's far from enough to enjoy the enchanting scenery just at the bottom of the mountain, isn't it? Therefore, a park was built against the Linping Mountain for people to have fun. The Linping Park has witnessed the happy childhood of countless people born in the 1980s and the 1990s. Now it's a popular rendezvous for lovers, parents with kids and retired people, square-dancing aunties are all enjoying their leisure time harmoniously in the park as well. The park was constantly being renovated, with the Azalea Park and Round Hill Trail opening to the public in 2023.

Fortunately, I used to climb the Linping Mountain in spring time. The time-honored and sky-covering luxuriant trees seemed to have evolved into the shelter of Linping Mountain, cooling you down once you stepped in. The sunlight dripped down through the leaves, being sacred and tranquil because of the Tyndall effect. It seemed that the story of *The Wizard of Oz* was unfolding along the mountain roads. The azaleas were just in time to bloom. Masses of azaleas in various colors filled the gaps between hillsides in unbroken lines. As a poem goes, "It is fortunate to find a worldly place in city without hustle and bustle but with mountains and forests one is deeply fond of." Linping Park indeed gives full play to the beauty of this kind.

Reading poems and allusions of the ancients all over the park, you will find that "yinyi," or "seclusion," truly describes the cultural essence of Linping Mountain. Heading towards Donglai Pavilion, I went uphill to a higher place and saw a Tang-style tower connected by metal mortise-and-tenon joints standing out, being both classical and modern. It's just as the poet Su Dongpo said, "Who is like the tower on Linping Mountain, greeting and seeing off visitors from high above?" I climbed the stairs and got to the top by a lift, to take a glimpse of the town consisting of buildings standing row upon row and side by side. At the top, the wind in April brought unexpected cool and birds chirped mystically from afar. The broad perspective and carefree transcendence overwhelmed me all at once.

东来阁
Donglai Pavilion

杭 州 临 平 大 剧 院

匠 心 之 门

爬过临平山，我惦记临平湖。临平山是老城的精神图腾，临平湖则是新城的文化地标。临平湖因在西湖之东，被改称"东湖"。现在的东湖，位置恰在临平南站之北，自然成了高铁旅客眼中的临平封面。

封面就得有封面的气势。映衬开阔湖面的，是临湖而建的"匠心之门"与临平大剧院。独特的冰裂纹造型和倾斜的房顶，让大剧院气质高雅而现代，没人能抵挡它的诱惑，它一建成便毫无悬念地成为网红"打卡"热点。这座拥有1200座大剧场、500座小剧场的建筑，一年的演出项目排得满满当当，夜晚的文化盛宴周周上演。

After climbing Linping Mountain, I kept thinking about "Linping Lake."
While Linping Mountain is the spiritual totem of the old city, Linping Lake
is the cultural landmark of the new one.

Located to the east of West Lake, Linping Lake was renamed as "East
Lake" (Donghu). The East Lake today is located right to the north of
Linping South Railway Station, naturally becoming the signature of Linping
like a cover of a book in the eyes of high-speed railway passengers.

A cover needs to show its momentum. What works in concert with the
open lake are the constructions called "Door of Ingenuity" and the Linping
Grand Theater nearby. The unique ice-crack style and sloping roof make
the theater elegant and modern. No one can resist its temptation, so the
theater undoubtedly became an Internet-famous site attracting visitors upon
its completion. In the building which includes a large theater with 1,200
seats and a small one with 500 seats, the programme is full all year round
and night cultural feasts are staged every week.

临平区文化馆
Linping Cultural Center

东湖之畔俨然是新城的文化聚集地，文艺时尚的气息透过大剧院奔涌而出，形成一整片滨湖的文艺空间。紧挨着大剧院，建有临平区文化馆。临品书坊是设在文化馆一楼的阅读场所，洁净而舒适，有交互式数字设备加持，是读书人难得的好去处。

Obviously, the culture of the new city gathers by the East Lake. The ambiance of literature and art gushes out of the theater, which creates a cultural world all around the lakeside. Next to the Linping Grand Theater is the Linping Cultural Center. Linpin Bookshop is a reading area on the first floor of the center. It is not only clean and cozy but also equipped with interactive digital devices, providing an excellent place for book lovers.

E-Fashion
艺尚小镇
Town

　　再往西走，是省级特色小镇——艺尚小镇。这座湖畔小镇的建成，恰是本地时尚产业的开花结果。低密度的建筑布局、肆意铺开的草地、看似随意的咖啡店外摆，时尚而松弛，与东湖的粼粼水纹互为呼应，无止境的畅想和生活情趣飘散在整个天空。

Moving westwards, you will see the E-Fashion Town, a characteristic town at provincial level. The completion of such a town by the lake is exactly the fruitful result brought by the local fashion industry. Low density constructions, unrestrained expansive grassland, and seemingly random outdoor seating areas of coffee shops are all fashionable and relaxing, echoing with the sparkling waves of the East Lake. Boundless imagination and the joy of life are flowing to the sky.

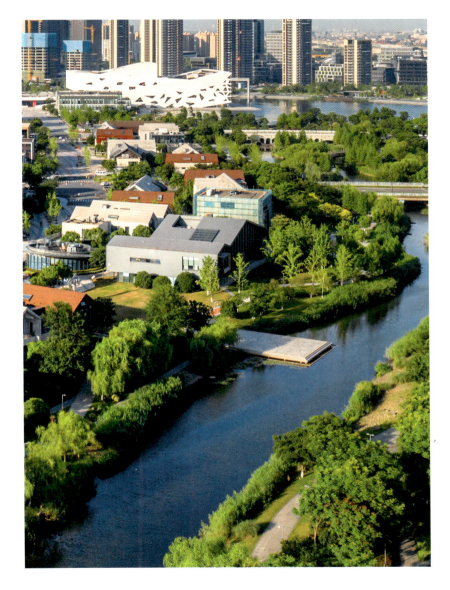

在小镇闲逛，浑然不觉时间流逝，还遇到几个熟悉的品牌。比如 INXX，杭州许多综合体里都有它家店铺；比如臻元箱包，它是北京冬奥会中国代表团唯一的行李箱供应商、杭州亚运会箱包特许生产企业；再比如李加林工作室，对，没错，它的主人就是那位多次用织锦制作国礼的大师。

工作日的下午，有些店铺在促销，有些店铺在上新，有些店铺在直播。直播带货早已成为服装销售的重要渠道。与艺尚小镇的服装时尚产业相匹配，临平新城升级了服装产业链，聚集了构美（浙江）信息科技有限公司、杭州谋事文化传媒有限公司等拥有抖音代运营资质的高质量数字化转型服务商，为更多实体企业提供品牌分析、直播间代运营、网红孵化、流量投放等全套服务。

Wandering in the town without even knowing the passage of time, I encountered several familiar brands. For instance, INXX, which set up shops in multiple commercial complexes of Hangzhou; Justreal, the exclusive suitcase supplier for the Chinese delegation during the Olympic Winter Games Beijing 2022 and the licensed manufacturer of bags and suitcases for the 19th Asian Games Hangzhou 2022; and Li Jialin Studio, the studio of the master as you know who turned brocade into state gifts multiple times.

On the weekday afternoon, some stores were promoting their products, some were launching new goods, and some were live-streaming, which has already been a major channel to sell clothes. To match the local fashion industry, Linping New City upgraded the industrial chain of clothing, and gathered

service providers with TikTok agency of operation for high-quality digitization, including Goumee (Zhejiang) Information Technology Co., Ltd., Hangzhou Moushi Culture Communication Co., Ltd. In doing so, more business entities can enjoy the whole set of services, including brand analysis, operation agency of live-streaming platforms, incubation of online celebrities, and advertising and marketing for more traffic.

AIRMETER 空刻
奶油培根配白葡萄提香意面
Creamy Bacon With White Wine Pasta

AIRMETER 空刻
黑胡椒牛柳意大利面
Black Pepper Beef Fillet Pasta

AIRMETER 空刻
经典番茄肉酱烩意大利面
Classic Tomato Bolognese Pasta

我在这里还偶遇了 2022 年抖音
意大利面的销售冠军——空刻意面。

Here I also encountered Airmeter, the bestseller of pasta on TikTok in 2022.

　　为实现产学研融合，艺尚小镇与中国美术学院和浙江理工大学等高校达成了长期合作。其中，浙江理工大学在临平设立了新校区，引入了服装学院、艺术与设计学院、国际时装技术学院、马兰戈尼时尚设计学院等与服装产业息息相关的专业。

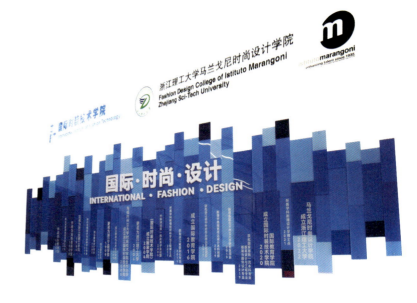

To realize industry−university−research integration, E-Fashion Town has signed long-term cooperative agreements with colleges and universities such as China Academy of Art, Zhejiang Sci-Tech University. In specific, Zhejiang Sci-Tech University established a new campus in Linping, bringing in fashion industry-related schools including the School of Fashion Design & Engineering, School of Art and Design, International Institute of Fashion Technology, and Fashion Design College of Istituto Marangoni.

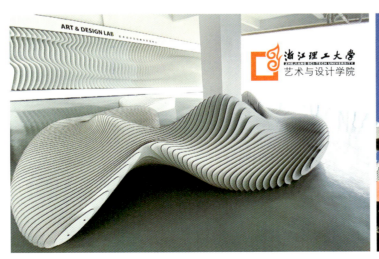

朱炳仁铜

銅熱

COPPER ART

创意无处不在，就是要颠覆日常。

　　文化创意产业正在成为临平发展的全新竞争力。杭州朱炳仁铜艺股份有限公司是临平另一家由非遗走向创意的文化制造企业。朱炳仁·铜品牌承袭于 1875 年始建的"朱府铜艺"，以朱府铜艺第四代传人、中国工艺美术大师朱炳仁名字命名。

　　2006 年，朱炳仁先生应邀为常州天宁宝塔镀铜衣，工程进行中发生了一些意外。他赶赴现场后发现，被火灼烧后流淌到地面的铜渣堆叠，迸发出一种无序而震撼的美感，由此创新出"熔铜"技术，铜从此成为一种可自由延展的材料。此后的十余年里，朱炳仁先生对熔铜技法的艺术表达进行了极其丰富的尝试，又在过程中创造了庚彩技艺、高温珐琅彩铜等新技艺。

　　朱炳仁先生因在运河申遗中作出的巨大贡献，又与古建筑学家罗哲文、郑孝燮并称"运河三老"。未来，随着大运河科创城的建设，我们能在塘栖古镇景区内看见朱炳仁大运河艺术馆的落成。

Creativity is everywhere as we think out of the box.

Cultural and creative industries are becoming the brand-new competitiveness of Linping. Hangzhou Zhu Bingren Copper Art Co., Ltd. is another cultural manufacturer in Linping designing cultural products based on intangible cultural heritage. The Zhu Bingren Copper is inherited from the Zhu Family Copper Art, which was established in 1875 and named after Zhu Bingren, the fourth descendant of the Zhu Family Copper Art and a Chinese master of arts and crafts.

In 2006, Mr. Zhu Bingren was invited to plate copper for the Tian Ning Pagoda in Changzhou city. In its process, something unexpected happened. He hurried to the site but found that the molten copper slag flowed onto the ground and piled up after burning, creating a kind of beauty featuring disorder and surprise. Then, the "copper melting" technique was created, and since then copper became a freely malleable material. Over the next decade, Mr. Zhu Bingren made various attempts to present the art of copper melting, and invented Gengcai technique (adding colorful paint to melted copper), high-temperature copper enameling technique and other new techniques.

Thanks to his great contribution to the application for World Heritage of Beijing–Hangzhou Grand Canal, Zhu Bingren was crowned alongside architects Luo Zhewen and Zheng Xiaoxie as "Three Elderly Contributors to the Grand Canal." With the development of the Science and Technology Innovation City along the Grand Canal, we are going to see the Zhu Bingren Grand Canal Gallery set up in the scenic area of Tangxi Ancient Town Scenic Area in the future.

朱炳仁铜艺所在的临平国家级经济技术开发区，成立于 1993 年，是杭州四大国家级开发区之一。这里聚焦高端装备制造、生物医药、新材料新能源、时尚布艺等主导产业，拥有春风动力、老板电器、贝达药业等 15 家上市公司。

Established in 1993, the Linping National Economic and Technological Development Zone, where Hangzhou Zhu Bingren Copper Art Co., Ltd. is located, is one of the four national development zones of Hangzhou. Focusing on leading industries of high-end equipment manufacturing, bio-medicine, new material and new energy, and fashion fabric, it is home to 15 listed companies including Zhejiang CFMOTO Power Co., Ltd., Hangzhou ROBAM Appliance Co., Ltd., Betta Pharmaceuticals Co., Ltd.

老板电器全球烹饪艺术中心
ROBAM International Cooking Art Center

浙江春风动力股份有限公司，沪市主板上市企业。其研发的国宾护卫摩托车（CF650G），集 27 项专利于一身，展现"中国制造""浙江创造"新形象，曾亮相于纪念抗战胜利 70 周年大阅兵。

ZHEJIANG CFMOTO POWER Co., Ltd. is a company listed in the main board market of the Shanghai Stock Exchange. The escort motorcycle CF650G developed by the company combines 27 patents in one product and showcases the new images of products "Made in China" and "Created in Zhejiang," which was debuted in the grand military parade to commemorate the 70th Anniversary of the Victory of the Chinese People's War of Resistance Against Japanese Aggression and the World Anti-fascist War.

杭州西奥电梯有限公司，经营业绩稳居国内品牌首位、行业前四位。曾因深达 102 米的京张高铁八达岭长城站使用其电梯而被广为报道。走进这里的"未来工厂"——电梯行业首家应用数字孪生技术的工厂，50 多条数字生产线、24 小时全面在线监测质量，达成 2 分钟生产 1 台电梯的超高效率，结合 5G、AI 等新一代前沿技术，西奥电梯实现智能制造自动化率近 100%。

XIO LIFT Co., Ltd. ranks first nationwide and fourth in world in terms of business performance. It was widely reported for its elevators operating at the 102-meter-deep Badaling Great Wall Station of the Beijing–Zhangjiakou High-speed Railway. In its "Future Factory," the first factory to apply digital twin technology in the elevator industry, over 50 digital production lines and 24/7 online quality monitoring make the productivity as superhigh as 1 elevator in 2 minutes. Combined with 5G, AI and other new cutting-edge technologies, the company is nearly 100% automatic.

杭州老板电器股份有限公司，深市主板上市企业。国内厨电行业的领导品牌，浙江数字化改革的样板企业，正致力于推动数字烹饪，这个变革让懒于烹饪又无法降低食物标准的人充满期待。

HANGZHOU ROBAM APPLIANCE Co., Ltd. is a company listed in the main board market of the Shenzhen Stock Exchange. As a domestic leader in the kitchen appliance industry and a business model advancing digital transformation in Zhejiang, the company is committed to facilitating digital cooking, which is something to look forward to for people like me who is too lazy to cook but still cannot compromise with unsavory food.

XIO LIFT 西奥电梯

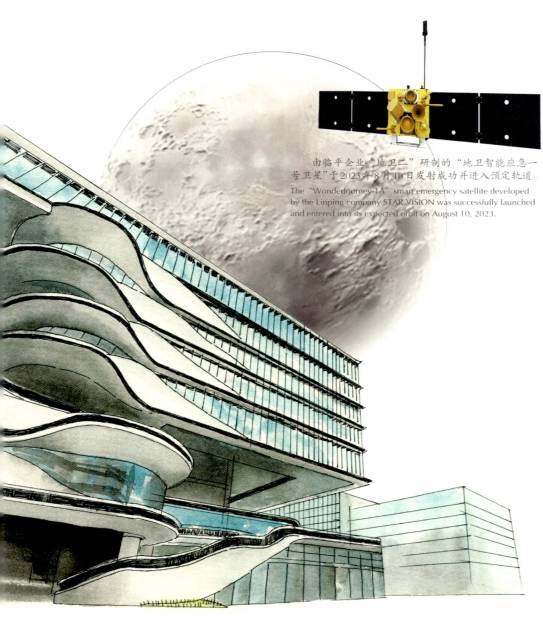

由临平企业"地卫二"研制的"地卫智能应急一号卫星"于2023年8月10日发射成功并进入预定轨道。
The "WonderJourney-1A" smart emergency satellite developed by the Linping company STAR.VISION was successfully launched and entered into its expected orbit on August 10, 2023.

临平的产业链布局是有谋略的，讲究供需对接、协作配套。经济技术开发区承接着诸多已实现数字化转型的"智"造企业，而数字化的关键在算力。聚焦数字化产业链的补链强链，临平适时推出了中国（杭州）算力小镇，进一步为数字产业发展赋能。算力小镇位于乔司街道，比邻丰收湖，从地理上看是临平向南"融杭"的第一站。自2021年12月开园至今，算力小镇引入地卫二空间技术（杭州）有限公司、杭州联芯通半导体有限公司等注册企业1000余家，实现营收约50亿元。

阿里云 supET 工业互联网创新中心
Alibaba Cloud supET Industrial Internet Innovation Center

地卫二空间技术（杭州）有限公司（STAR. VISION）是一家全球化太空智能卫星公司，其技术团队是我国最早使用工业级元器件研制卫星的团队。在 2022 年美国电气与电子工程师协会国际计算机视觉与模式识别会议上，地卫二在地球与环境多模态挑战赛中获得 2 项亚军及 1 项多国数据集冠军，是唯一获奖的航天企业。地卫二的加入，让临平可以天上地下一起算。

The layout of the industrial chain in Linping is strategic, which focuses on the balance between supply and demand, as well as industry support and coordination. The Linping National Economic and Technological Development Zone is home to multiple already digitized intelligent manufacturers. Besides, the key to digitization is computing power. With the focus on the complementary and strong parts of the digital industrial chain, Linping timely launched the China Town of Computing Power to further empower the digital industry. Located in Qiaosi Subdistrict and next to the Fengshou Lake, it is geographically the first station for Linping to "integrate with Hangzhou" southwards. Since opened in December of 2021, it has attracted over 1,000 registered enterprises such as STAR.VISION Aerospace Group Limited and Hangzhou Unicom Semiconductor Co., Ltd., generating revenue of about RMB 5 billion.

STAR.VISION is an international company of space intelligent satellites, whose technical team is the first to use industrial components and parts to develop satellites in China. In CVPR 2022 held by IEEE, the company won second place twice in MultiEarth 2022 and took the crown once in Multinational Data Set respectively, being the only aerospace enterprise on the list. The settlement of STAR.VISION enables Linping to have computing power on earth and in space.

同样位于乔司街道的宜家家居（杭州店），自 2015 年开张至今，已有 8 年了。

Ikea (Hangzhou Store), which is also located at Qiaosi Subdistrict, has been operated for 8 years since its opening in 2015.

临平文化艺术长廊
Culture and Art Corridor

正是因为有如此强大的产业链支撑，临平的繁华街区已是楼厦林立，成熟的商圈熠熠生辉。走在一个如此富足的城市里，和文化相遇是一件必然的事情，在剧院，在书摊，在咖啡店，在每个意想不到的小巷深处。但这里的文化养成远不止于自然生长。临平区的文化艺术长廊，就是一个精心规划、专业管理的高品质开放式文化场馆。长廊南北贯通，北接临平山，南临上塘河，由老城有机更新而来，建有戏曲艺术交流中心、图书馆、文化艺术交流中心三组建筑，兼顾"一老一小"市民曲艺欣赏、阅读、表演等文化需求。一早一晚，只要天气好，文化艺术长廊都是热闹的，爱戏曲、爱排舞的阿姨们都会自发来"打卡"交流，接受文艺与友情的双重洗礼，滋养心中的生命之光。

Supported by such a strong industrial chain, Linping has already built up busy blocks bristling with high-rises and shining business circles. Walking in such a wealthy city, it's natural to encounter culture events in theaters, at bookstalls, in coffee shops, or in any unexpected deep alleys. The culture here is cultivated far more than just letting everything take its course. The Culture and Art Corridor of Linping District is a well-planned and professionally managed open cultural venue of high quality. The corridor runs north and south, connecting Linping Mountain with Shangtang River. Renovated from the old city, it consists of the Opera and Art Exchange Center, a library, and the Culture and Art Exchange Center, meeting the demand of both the elderly and young to appreciate opera, read, and perform. As long as weather permitted, the corridor will always be busy both in the morning and evening. Aunties who love opera or dance will come spontaneously to communicate with each other, and receive the dual baptism of art and friendship.

临平智慧图书馆
Linping Smart Library

戏曲艺术交流中心
Opera and Art Exchange Center

临平上塘河上，有两座桥作为经典地标，见证过无数临平人的来往故事。

Over the Shangtang River in Linping, there are two bridges as classic landmarks, which have witnessed the comings and goings of countless Linping people.

桂芳桥

南北向横跨上塘河的单孔石桥，2013 年作为中国大运河水系的一部分，被列为全国重点文物保护单位。

Guifang Bridge

It's a single-hole stone bridge across the Shangtang River from south to north, and it was listed as a key cultural relics site under the propection of the state in 2013 as part of the Grand Canal system of China.

隆兴桥

始建年代不详，但能查到宋天禧年间 (1017—1021) 重修，清乾隆二十七年 (1762) 重建。它也是南北向跨上塘河的单孔石拱桥，属于杭州市市级文物保护单位。

Longxing Bridge

The date of its construction is unknown, but it can be found that it was renovated in the Tianxi period of Song Dynasty (1017-1021) and rebuilt in the 27th year of Qianlong of Qing Dynasty (1762). It is also a south to north single-hole stone arch bridge over the Shangtang River, and a municipal cultural relics protection site in Hangzhou.

散落老城区的口袋公园，不仅是以高品质空间点亮百姓生活的重要抓手，更是叠加诸多功能的高效公共空间。

The pocket parks scattered in the old city serve not only as high-quality space to light up people's life but also efficient public areas with multiple functions.

康养文化口袋公园
公园以一道结合健康养生为主题的景墙为特色。

Health and Wellness Culture Pocket Park
It features a landscape wall that combines the theme of health and wellness.

瓶山文化口袋公园
"瓶山"即"酒瓶堆如山"。临平怎么会堆着那么多酒瓶呢？一种说法是南宋抗金将领在此犒劳士兵，豪饮后酒瓶堆积如山；另一种说法是这里曾经是宋代朝廷设立的酒类市场和征税管理机构。不管怎样，公园以大量酒瓶为设计元素，与宋代酒文化遥相呼应。

Pingshan Culture Pocket Park
"Pingshan" means "bottle mountain," and why are so many bottles piled up in Linping? One saying is that anti-Jin generals in the Southern Song Dynasty rewarded soldiers here, and bottles piled up after soldiers drinking heavily; another saying is that this place was once a wine market and also taxation administrations were established here in the Song Dynasty. In any case, a large number of wine bottles are used in the park as its design element, which echoes the wine culture of the Song Dynasty.

牛拖船口袋公园
公园的主题"牛拖船"，起源于清末民初，为临平所特有。一般是一头牛拖 6—7 艘小船，由一人在船头驾牛牵船指引方向，另一人手拿竹篙在船上机动作业，防止船转弯时碰岸碰桥。这种运输方式已消失近半个世纪。

Ox-towed Boat Park
The theme of the park—Ox-towed-boat was originated in the late Qing Dynasty and the early Republic of China, which is unique to Linping. Generally, an ox towed 6—7 boats, and one person drove the ox in the bow to guide the boat, while another held a bamboo pole to maneuver so as to prevent the boat from bumping the shore or bridge when turning. This mode of transportation has been gone for nearly half a century.

纵然生活舒心惬意，临平也从不缺速度与激情。土生土长的临平本地运动——滚灯，于 2016 年入选第一批国家非物质文化遗产名录，2023 年 2 月入选杭州亚运会、亚残会开闭幕式暖场节目资源库。滚灯被戏称为我国古代"黑科技"，在江南多地都有分布，外部是竹片围成的球形竹笼，内部中空，另有两个小圆圈立体交叉，球心装有点燃的蜡烛。无论外部的竹笼怎样翻滚，内部由类似万象支撑固定的蜡烛都不会翻倒熄灭，十分有趣。临平的滚灯表演中，演员需配合音乐起伏节奏，让数十斤重的竹球滚灯像皮球一样在自身的周围上下翻飞，极富阳刚之美，又有浑然天成的江南气韵。

Besides comfortable and cozy life, Linping also never lacks speed and passion. Rolling Lamp, an indigenous sport of Linping, was included in the first batch of the National Intangible Cultural Heritage List in 2016. This February, Rolling Lamp was selected in the warm-up program library for the opening ceremonies of the 19th Asian Games Hangzhou 2022 and the 4th Asian Para Games Hangzhou 2022. Rolling Lamp is dubbed black technology of ancient China, being distributed widely in the Jiangnan region south of the Yangtze River. The lamp is composed of an external bamboo cage in ball shape, and hollowed internal structure with two 3D intersected circles inside and a lighted candle at the center. It's quite interesting that no matter how the external bamboo cage rolls, the candle never overturns or extinguishes as if being supported by everything around it. In the Rolling Lamp performance, performers should roll the tens-of-jin (500g for 1 jin) lamp up and down like a ball with the music, featuring both the beauty of masculinity and the natural charm of Jiangnan.

悦悦
Yueyue

临临
Linlin

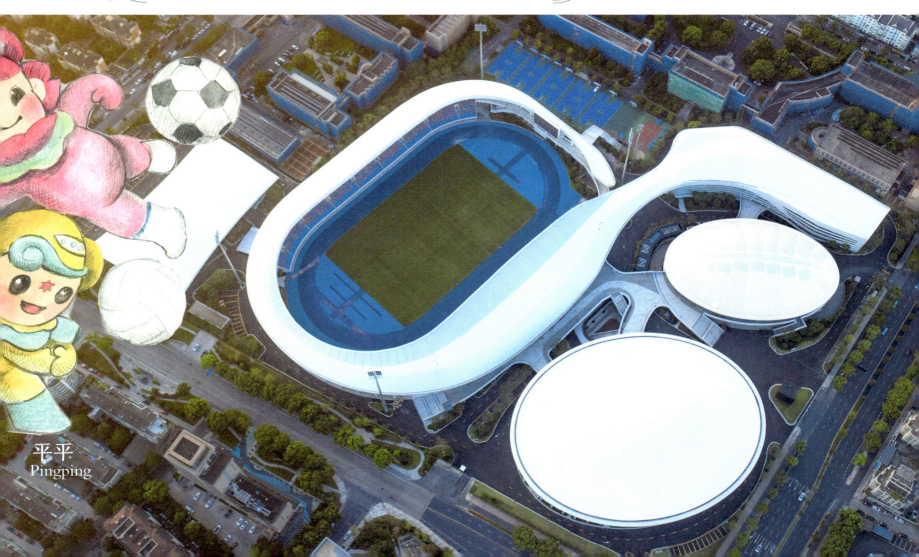

平平
Pingping

临平体育中心

借着亚运的东风，临平人的健身场馆得到了国际化、智能化、无障碍化提升。新建的临平体育中心，总建筑面积约9.5万平方米，含体育馆、体育场、游泳馆、综合训练馆和风雨操场等五大场馆，将在亚运期间承接足球、排球、空手道等多项赛事。白天，这里升腾着运动与科技带来的欢悦；夜晚，馆群的轮廓灯带点亮，柔和变幻的色彩还原出设计师"丝绸之路"的设计理念，灵动的曲线流淌出江南的柔美意境。

改造提升后的场馆，配备了一颗数字"心"。体育馆的标准时钟、场地扩声、LED 显示屏、360 度斗屏、影像采集回放等都使用智能化系统，能够为观众带来更好的观看体验；消控指挥中心使用的智慧化系统，使后台工作人员能实时掌握前方动态，精准高效处置突发事件；主场馆的灯光可以通过系统实现节日模式设定、平日模式设定、节能模式设定等一键切换，节能又高效。

Seizing opportunities brought by the Asian Games, the sports venues of Linping are improved to be more international, smarter, and more barrier-free. Covering about 95,000 square meters in total, the new Linping Sports Center includes 5 venues as a gymnasium, a stadium, a natatorium, a comprehensive training center, and a storm-proof playground, which will stage games of football, volleyball, karate, etc. during the Asian Games. In the daytime, people enjoy the happiness brought by technologies and sports here; in the evening, the lighted contour lights of venues explain the design philosophy of "Silk Road" with soft and shifting colors and picture the gentle beauty of Jiangnan with flexible curves.

After renovation, the venues are equipped with digital "hearts." The standard clock, microphone, LED screen, 360-degree funnel-shaped screen, image capture and playback of the gymnasium are all smart to provide better viewing experience for the audience. The smart system of Fire Control and Command Center enables back-stage staff members to stay current with real-time situations in the gym, and cope with emergencies in targeted and effective ways. The lights of main venues can switch to festival mode, regular mode, or energy-saving mode via a simple press, being both energy-saving and efficient.

此外，位于星桥的杭州跑步中心也是一个颇具人气的网红运动"打卡"地。相比于体育中心，这是一块更有野趣的开放式综合健身场地，除了室外跑道、室内球馆，还设有户外卡丁车、农业研学观光园等，时不时有彩色铁皮火车在场地里高高架起的铁路上呼啸而过，和你赛跑。春风乍起时，春草茸茸，星星点点的小花绽放，这里真是风筝与露营的天堂。

跑步
中心

Besides, the Hangzhou Running Center on Xingqiao Subdistrict is also a quite popular Internet-famous sports field. Compared with Linping Sports Center, it is an open comprehensive body-building field enjoying more rustic charm. Besides an indoor arena, it also has outdoor synthetic racetracks, an karting track, an agricultural sightseeing garden, and so on. Frequently，there are colorful iron-clad trains that roar past along the highly elevated railway and race with you. As the spring breeze comes, clusters of flowers will scatter and bloom on the soft grassland, creating a paradise for kite flying and camping.

杭州跑步中心
Hangzhou Running Center

说到星桥，地理上它横跨上塘河两岸，北岸多山丘。南宋时，它是京畿门户，设有斑荆馆（相当于给金国等来使的"国宾馆"）。延续了这里曾经沟通内外的基因，今天许多在杭州的外国朋友都会来星桥"打卡"——只为一睹"小巴黎"的小埃菲尔铁塔。小埃菲尔铁塔按巴黎埃菲尔铁塔 1：3 缩放制作，矗立在天都城广场上，它身后是一条长长的带状喷泉花园，直通向由罗马广场和数百级台阶架起在高处的天都公园正门，这样的景象真的会让人联想到巴黎。天都公园开放于 2002 年，是一座占地 1000 亩的法兰西风情主题公园，内有山顶城堡、天鹅湖、仿凡尔赛宫纳特尔公园建造的宫廷花园，天鹅湖边的沙滩是孩子的乐园。湖的附近则是一个婚纱拍摄基地，在公园里随处可见婚纱拍摄团队。

天都城
Tianducheng

Speaking of Xingqiao Subdistrict, it stretches across
the Shangtang River geographically to the mountainous north bank.
In the Southern Song Dynasty, it was the gate of the capital city and its environs,
with the establishment of the Banjing Guan (equal to the "State Guesthouse" for envoys from
the State of Jin). Renewing its gene to connect people at home and abroad, today Xingqiao Subdistrict
continues to be a popular site attracting foreign friends in Hangzhou. Many of them come especially for the
Tianducheng Eiffel Tower. Standing in Tianducheng Square, the tower is scaled down to 1/3 the size of the original one.
Behind it, there is a long band-shaped fountain garden leading straightforward to the Tianducheng Roman Forum and the front
gate of Tiandu Park highly elevated by hundreds of steps, which tends to remind people of the real Paris. Opened in 2002, Tiandu
Park is a French-style theme park covering 1,000 mu (667 square meters for 1 mu), consisting of a hilltop castle, a swan lake, and a palace
garden from the model of the Natal Park of Château de Versailles, etc. Moreover, the sand beach by the swan lake is a fairground for children.
Beside the lake, there is a wedding photography base in which camera crews are everywhere.

　　天都公园背靠着的，是临平另一个隐逸文化的代表——黄鹤山。元代山水画的代表为"元四家"。元四家之一的王蒙曾在黄鹤山隐居 30 年，自号黄鹤山樵。隐居生活是王蒙画作非常重要的表现主题，比如现藏于台北故宫博物院的《黄鹤草堂图》，就是他隐居黄鹤山后，由此处山水而产生的"心相"。受此启发，已经有地产公司在黄鹤山按王蒙画作展开美学造盘，营建的是当代人最珍视的低密度如画山水人居。

At the back of Tiandu Park is Huanghe Mountain, another epitome of the hermit culture of Linping. The "Four Masters of the Yuan Dynasty" are four representatives of landscape painting of the Yuan Dynasty. Wang Meng, a member of the Four Masters, lived in Huanghe Mountain as a hermit for 30 years and styled himself as "a woodman in Huanghe Mountain." Life in seclusion is a very significant theme of his composition. For instance, the *Picture of Huanghe Cottage* now in the Taipei Palace Museum captures his "state of mind" cultivated by local mountains and waters. Enlightened by this, some real estate companies have already started to develop the region based on Wang Meng's artworks to construct land-extensive and picturesque houses that are most cherished today.

REVIEW THE OLD DREAM AND CREATE THE NEW ALONGSIDE THE GRAND CANAL

运河边，温旧梦，造新梦

2006 年诺贝尔文学奖获得者作家帕慕克写他的故乡伊斯坦布尔，在题记中，他说："美景之美，在其忧伤。"作为财富曾经流转的重要通道，后因铁路运输兴起而式微淡出，运河无疑是美而忧伤的。但运河之于临平，远不只是人们重温文脉、凭吊往事的梦里水乡。大运河遗产的保护传承利用在临平有了新的载体——临平大运河国家文化公园暨临平大运河科创城，作为重构河畔发展格局的产业平台，文化与科创在此跨界碰撞出新的火花，孕育出城市的诗和远方。

While writing about his homeland Istanbul, Orhan Pamuk, the writer who won Nobel Literature Prize in 2006, said in the epigraph, "The beauty of scenery resides in its sorrow." The beauty of the Beijing–Hangzhou Grand Canal also resides in its sorrow because the Canal used to be a major channel of transport but started to decline since the rise of railway transportation. However, for Linping, the Canal creates far more than just a dream hometown to review previous culture and memories. The protection, inheritance, and utilization of the heritage of the Beijing–Hangzhou Grand Canal take a new shape in Linping, namely the Grand Canal (Linping section) National Cultural Park & the Grand Canal (Linping section) Science and Technology Innovation City. As an industrial platform to restructure the development pattern along the canal, it produces a new spark via trans-boundary collision of culture and scientific and technological innovation and creates the poetic life in the city.

塘栖古镇（国家 AAAA 级景区）是临平
运河文化一个活的印证。

　　塘栖得名于"沿塘而栖"，明清时已是
富甲一方，贵为"江南十大名镇"之首。

The ancient town Tangxi (National AAAA Level
Tourist Attraction) is a vivid epitomize of the Canal
culture of Linping.

The ancient town Tangxi was named after
"yantangerqi," or "dwelling along the canal." In
Ming and Qing Dynasties, it has already developed
into a wealthy town, being the top of "10 Well-
known Towns of Jiangnan."

运河蜿蜒流经众多码头，塘栖何以能破圈而出，成为东出杭州的运河重镇呢？

上塘河水悠悠，千年来曾载过无数南来北往的贵胄、商贾，但随着明代江南经济的发展，10米宽的上塘河古道显然不够用了；经过当年的专家论证，元末新开挖疏浚了一条从塘栖到杭州的下塘河，因为沿途本就有很多天然小湖泊，河道宽达100米，运力提升了好几倍，来往的大宗货物与人流量一下子就上了好几个台阶。

今天我们走高速，大都每隔50千米有一个服务区；同样的道理，当年走运河，五六十里是一个节点，一般船行五六十里会停下来，歇脚过夜。上塘河从杭州古艮山门到临平为五六十里，因此古上塘河时代造就了临平镇（今临平街道）的繁荣；下塘河从杭州武林门到塘栖也为五六十里，加上塘栖东接桐乡、嘉兴，北通德清、湖州，这样一个位置，自然成长为一个新的黄金码头。

The Canal meanders through numerous wharves, then how can Tangxi stand out and evolve into a major canal town east out of Hangzhou?

Shangtang River flows without haste. Though carrying countless members of the nobility and merchants between south and north over the past thousands of years, the 10-meter-wide ancient river-way was evidently no longer enough to meet the demand of economic growth in Jiangnan during the Ming Dynasty. After experts' argumentation, the Xiatang River from Tangxi to Hangzhou was dredged out in the later Yuan Dynasty. Thanks to multiple natural lakes all along, the river-way reached 100 meters and its carrying capacity multiplied, thus the traffic of commodities and passengers embracing leapfrog development immediately.

Driving on the expressway today, you will see a service area every 50 km. Similarly, sailing on the canal, you would also see a rest station for overnight accommodation every 50 to 60 li in the past (500 m for 1 li). Shangtang River stretched 50 to 60 li from the ancient Genshan Gate of Hangzhou to Linping, therefore Linping Town (today's Linping Subdistrict) grew into a prosperous place in the ancient Shangtang River era. Xiatang River also expanded 50 to 60 li from Wulin Gate of Hangzhou to Tangxi. Besides, with Tongxiang and Jiaxing in the east as well as Deqing and Huzhou in the north, Tangxi was cultivated into a new golden wharf.

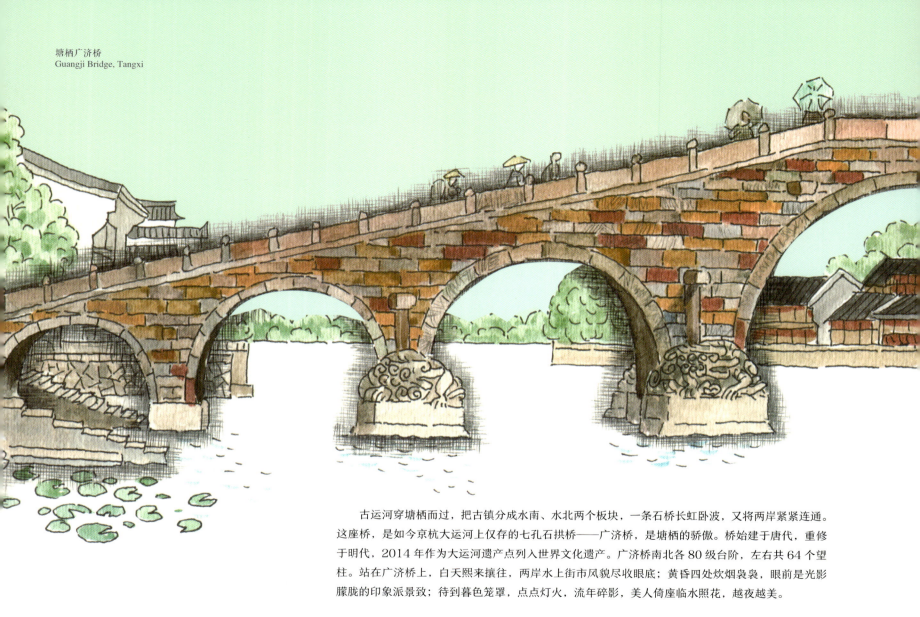

塘栖广济桥
Guangji Bridge, Tangxi

　　古运河穿塘栖而过，把古镇分成水南、水北两个板块，一条石桥长虹卧波，又将两岸紧紧连通。这座桥，是如今京杭大运河上仅存的七孔石拱桥——广济桥，是塘栖的骄傲。桥始建于唐代，重修于明代，2014年作为大运河遗产点列入世界文化遗产。广济桥南北各80级台阶，左右共64个望柱。站在广济桥上，白天熙来攘往，两岸水上街市风貌尽收眼底；黄昏四处炊烟袅袅，眼前是光影朦胧的印象派景致；待到暮色笼罩，点点灯火，流年碎影，美人倚座临水照花，越夜越美。

The ancient canal flows through Tangxi, dividing the town into south and north parts. A stone bridge named Guangji Bridge stands across the river and connects both sides. Guangji Bridge is the only seven-hole stone arch bridge existing over the Beijing–Hangzhou Grand Canal today as the pride of Tangxi. Built in the Tang Dynasty and renovated in the Ming Dynasty, Guangji Bridge was listed on the list of World Cultural Heritage as a part of the Grand Canal. The Guangji Bridge has 80 steps both in the north and south, and 64 pillars both on the left and right. 80 steps both in the north and south, and 64 pillars both on the left and right. Standing on the bridge, in the day, you will see passers-by on busy streets of both sides; at twilight, with smoke curling up from kitchens, you will see the hazy picture of impressionism; in the evening, you will see twinkling lights and mottled shadows of the beauty leaning on the chair in the water, and deeper at night the more beautiful the scenery will be.

这座铜像立于桥南，是明代宁波人陈守清。当年他从宁波来塘栖做生意时，运河上旧桥已毁，来往两岸全靠渡船。每逢天气恶劣，总有人落水溺亡。陈守清看不下去了，发愿修桥。为募集资金，他剃掉头发，像僧人一样游走四方，最后在京城感动了太后。在皇家的支持下，广济桥得以建成。

What stands on the south of the bridge is the bronze statue of Chen Shouqing, a Ningboer in the Ming Dynasty. When he came to Tangxi from Ningbo to do business, the old bridge over the river was damaged. Thus people crossed the river entirely by ferryboat. When the weather was bad, some people were drowned. Chen Shouqing couldn't bear that anymore and vowed to build a bridge. To raise money, he shaved his hair, lobbied here and there, and finally moved the Empress Dowager. With royal support, Guangji Bridge was built.

古运河如果有记忆，渗在她肌理中的故事未必能挨个数清，我只取一瓢饮，说说水北街御碑的故事。乾隆帝南巡，曾在塘栖下船御游，并得知一个重要消息：隔壁的江苏和安徽两省积欠朝廷巨款，浙江却已全数缴纳皇银。龙心大悦的皇帝当即下诏免了浙江30万税银，并刻下御碑表彰浙江官员办事得力。这块御碑目前完整地保存在古镇水北街的御碑码头。

If the ancient canal has its own memory, then her stories might cannot be fully elaborated. I will just pick one out to talk about the imperial monument in Shuibei Street. During his tour in the south, Emperor Qianlong once took a boat in Tangxi and was informed that while Jiangsu and Anhui Provinces had their debts to the royal government piling up, their neighbor Zhejiang Province had already paid the full amount. The Emperor was so satisfied that he issued an imperial edict to exempt the 300,000-tael tax of Zhejiang, and inscribed the imperial monument to commend Zhejiang officials' good performance. At present, the monument is still preserved intact at the Imperial Monument Wharf, Shuibei Street, Tangxi Ancient Town.

御碑码头
Imperial Monument Wharf

紧挨广济桥北端的水北街是今天塘栖古镇最重要的一条街，保留着大多数人想象中的经典水乡古镇风光，河街并行的格局、跫音回响的石板、连廊荫蔽的美人靠，一一存留至今。

The Shuibei Street right at the north end of Guangji Bridge is one of the most important streets of Tangxi Ancient Town today, reserving the classic scenery of waterside towns as imagined by most people. The layout of river and streets in parallel, slab-stones with echoing footfalls, and the Meirenkao Chairs along the corridors here all remain even till today.

美人靠
Meirenkao Chairs (a kind of Chinese traditional bench with lazyback which wins its name for being sit by beauties)

清水丝绵
Rinsing Silk Wadding

清末，因水路畅通，杭州、湖州的富商在水北街兴建了丝厂、绸厂、织布厂，开创了浙江民族资本工业的先河，也使这里成为浙江蚕丝工业的重镇。如今，工厂早已湮没，素来栽桑养蚕的塘栖倒是保留下了清水丝棉制作技艺，作为中国传统蚕桑丝织技艺的重要组成部分，2009 年经联合国教科文组织批准列入"人类非物质文化遗产代表作名录"。丝绵轻柔又保暖，一旦用过大都会爱上。水北街上的清水丝绵铺里，你总能看见当地的老阿婆三四人一起合着节奏默契地拉着丝绵，老阿婆们对于熟悉的女红有发自内心的热爱，她们的手工让整条街道充满暖意。一张洁白柔滑的丝绵，需经养蚕、选茧、煮茧、漂洗、剥丝、撑扯等道道工序才能得到，多张丝绵才能做成透气柔软的绵衣、绵被，其中牺牲了多少蚕宝宝的生命，耗费了多少人的心血。每每使用起来，免不了令人想起"一丝一缕，恒念物力维艰"。

In the late Qing Dynasty, blessed with unimpeded waterways, wealthy merchants of Hangzhou and Huzhou built to produce silk fabrics and other textile on Shuibei Street, making groundbreaking endeavors in establishing Zhejiang's national capital industries and turning Tangxi into a significant town of the silk industry. Nowadays, though the factories have already been shut down, Tangxi inherits the manufacturing craftsmanship of rinsing silk wadding which was as an important part of "China sericulture and silk weaving" included in the Masterpieces of the Intangible Heritage of Humanity by UNESCO in 2009. The silk wadding is both soft and warm, thus people always fall in love with it once using it. In silk wadding stores on Shuibei Street, you can always see 3 to 4 aunties cooperating very well in spinning. They have heartfelt passions for the familiar needlework, and their handicrafts warm the whole street. A piece of white and smooth silk wadding will take shape after procedures from silkworm breeding, cocoon picking, cocoon boiling, rinsing, and stripping, to stretching. Multiple pieces are required to make an air-permeable and soft coat or quilt. The costs of silkworms and labor are too high to measure. Whenever using it, people will be reminded of "the arduous efforts to produce each thread."

小米蒸糕
Steamed Millet Cake

椒桃片
Spicy Salt Traditional Flake Cake

桂花年糕
Osmanthus Sugar Rice Cakes

　　富裕年代总是会留下甜味的回忆。古朴的塘栖，如大多数古镇一样，拥有本地品牌传承百年的甜食。水北街上，门头最显眼的是白墙黑字卖藕粉糖色的聚源昌，但游客最先到达的，却是开在广济桥桥头的朱一堂和法根糕点。这两家作为本地糕点品牌的老字号，因价格公道、用料讲究，店里总是人群熙攘、生意热闹，各色酥糖、芝麻糖、椒桃片、大麻饼、桂花糖年糕，还有那带着几缕玫瑰花瓣的蒸糕在柜台一字排开，让人只看一眼多巴胺就已经开始溢出。对黏糯的迷恋，是江南水乡一种趋同的嗜好，我亦无力抗拒。写到这里，我情不自禁拿起手机，找到电商下单。

冰皮饼
Ice Crust Cake

枇杷梗
Pipa Geng(a kind of fried dessert)

桔红糕
Red Chinese Pastry with Orange Flavour

聚
源
昌
糖
色
藕
粉

In the age of plenty, there is always something sweet in memory. As most ancient towns do, the simple and unsophispicated Tangxi town has also developed its own centenary cake and pastry brands. In Shuibei Street, Juyuanchang, the store of lotus root starch, enjoys the most conspicuous storefront signboard consisting of white wall and black characters, while the first stores tourists reach are Zhuyitang Cake and Fagen Cake at the end of Guangji Bridge. As time-honored brands of local cakes and pastries, with the advantages of affordable price and high quality, the two stores are always filled with customers. Various crunchy candies, sesame candies, spicy salt traditional flake cake, sesame pancakes, osmanthus sugar rice cakes, and steamed cakes with rose petals are all displayed in line at the counter. Only a glance will release your dopamine. Most people in Jiangnan love the sticky flavor, and I'm no exception. Before continuing writing, I cannot help ordering some takeouts on my phone.

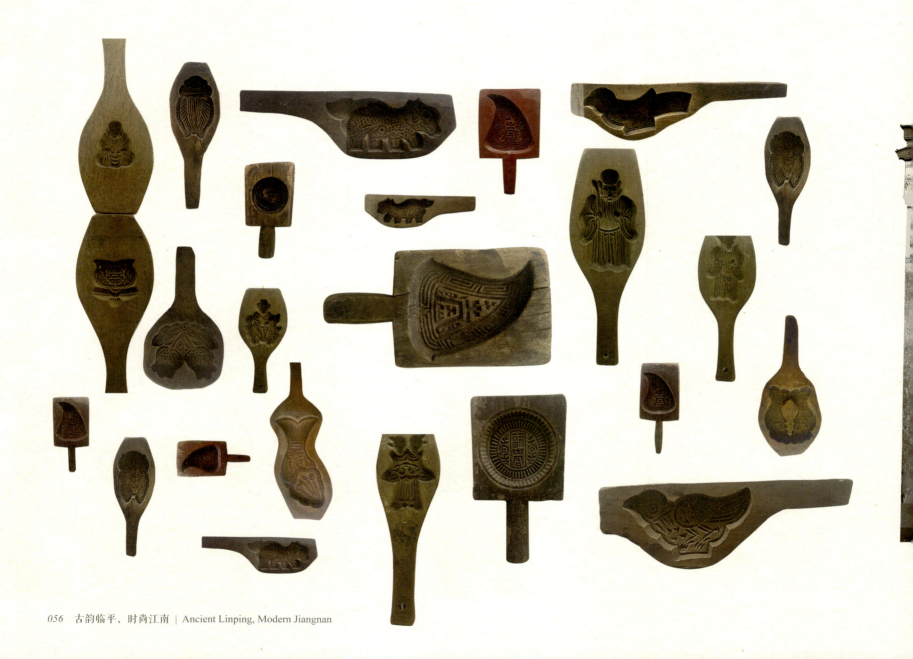

江楠糕版艺术馆
Jiangnan Cake and Pastry Mold Art Museum

在江南人的生活里，糕点不仅配茶食用，更是与节气习俗、生活礼俗紧密相连。青团见证清明的思念，麒麟糕与凤凰糕见证一户人家弄璋弄瓦的喜庆，鲤鱼年糕则见证年年有余、阖家团圆的幸福……如今办喜事用糕点的人少了，但制作糕点的老模具——糕模——却在这里变成了珍藏，得到了传承。塘栖古镇的糕模馆、超山的江楠糕版艺术馆，都收藏着不同地域、不同年代的木制模型，在陈列柜中无声胜有声地传递着它们曾经见过的人间故事。

For people living in Jiangnan, cakes and pastries are not only tea-mates, but also tightly relevant to customs. The Sweet Green Rice Ball witnesses people cherishing the memory with the deceased on Tomb-sweeping Day, Kylin Cake and Phoenix Cake witness the jubilant childbirth in a family, and carp rice cake witnesses the happy life of plenty and reunion. Nowadays, though fewer people are preparing for joyful events with cakes and pastries, whose old molds have become treasuries and have been inherited here. The Cake and Pastry Mold Museum in Tangxi Ancient Town and the Jiangnan Cake and Pastry Mold Art Museum in Chaoshan Scenic Area collect wooden molds from different places and of different ages. In display cabinets, the molds are telling the stories that they have seen in the world as if silence speaks.

汇昌大肉粽
Sticky Pork
Rice Dumplings
Produced by
Huichang

塘栖甜食中最广为流传的，是蜜饯。早年塘栖可以说是"家家户户做蜜饯，门前门后晒蜜饯"。清康熙年间张之鼐所著《栖里景物略》中有记载："（塘栖糖色）……京省驰名。"也就是说，康熙年间的塘栖蜜饯，已是享誉中央各部的美食了。到了近代上海开埠，社交生活催生出对零食的巨大需求，上海的冠生园、梅林等食品公司纷纷到塘栖找作坊做"代加工"，再贩售到全国各地，那是过去的辉煌。之后塘栖蜜饯一直自豪地保持着杭派蜜饯的代表身份，经历了传统工艺与现代技术的交融重生，已有 40 余家规模化的蜜饯生产加工企业，在全国占有行业的三分天下，年销售额达 30 多亿元人民币，诞生了如华味亨等规模化生产的大品牌。

古镇上的"百年汇昌"是塘栖蜜饯产业 400 多年发展史的见证者。作为早于胡庆余堂、知味观的杭州著名老商号，百年汇昌始创于 1800 年，原称"汇昌南北货栈"。清道光年间，其所产蜜饯、蜡烛被选为贡品；清光绪年间，"汇昌"成为内务府的指定供货商；1929 年首届西湖博览会，"汇昌"的桂花姜等蜜饯产品获得"特等奖"，也就是当时的最高奖。

百年汇昌现在的店铺位于水北街与西石塘街的交叉位置。门边坐着一位阿姨，不停地包着粽子，你只需扫一眼肉馅儿和粽叶，就能看出来成品尺寸一定特别大，普通人一个吃下去定能管饱；店铺里陈列各色糕饼、蜜饯，还有枇杷花，都是朴素的老式包装；看到里面深处，墙上挂着装裱起来"塘栖会馆"四个字，下面放着"塘栖镇虞铭理论宣讲工作室"的牌子。原来这里的掌柜姓虞，是面相和善的小镇"故事家"。

我多问了几句，又恰好客人不多，掌柜就泡上一壶茶给我讲起了塘栖故事。早年依赖京杭大运河，这里吸引了四面八方的人来此经商，而且不同地方的人盘踞在此，各自占领了一个行业："食物链"顶端的是徽州人，开当铺做金融；宁波人做糕饼；慈溪人做药材；江苏丹阳人做面粉；绍兴人做老酒；做泥水匠的肯定是东阳人……掌柜讲祖上从宁波来到塘栖的谋生经历，讲百年汇昌、翁长春两个老字号的人事变迁，讲当代塘栖镇上富豪的起起落落，最后还慷慨地分享了一下他的糕模珍藏。听毕，我不由得感叹，这一小时说的尽是世态悲欢、人生起落，事如芳草春常在，人似浮云影不留，人还是应该多努力做些能惠及世间的实在好事。

Preserved fruit is the most popular sweetmeat of Tangxi. In early times, literally "each household in Tangxi makes preserved fruit and dry it at both front and back doors." As recorded in *Introduction of Scenery and Things of Tangxi* by Zhang Zhinai in the Kangxi period of the Qing Dynasty, "Tangxi sweetmeat are well-known in the Jingsheng." That is to say, it has already gained high popularity in imperial government. In modern times when Shanghai opened commercial ports, social life created and catalyzed the great demand for snacks. Food companies in Shanghai including Shanghai Guanshengyuan Food Ltd. and Shanghai Maling Aquarius Co., Ltd. came to Tangxi one after another to look for original material manufacturers and then sold their products nationwide. Though the glory was left in the past, still as a representative of Hangzhou-style preserved fruit, Tangxi preserved fruit revived through the integration between traditional and modern techniques. In Tangxi, there are over 40 large-scale preserved fruit producers and manufacturers, accounting for one-third of the whole industry domestically and generating an annual revenue of over RMB 3 billion. In specific, there are big brands like Hangzhou Huaweiheng Biotechnology Co., Ltd. and so forth.

The "Centennial Huichang" in Tangxi has witnessed the development of the local preserved fruit industry over the past 400 years. Established earlier than time-honored brands such as Hangzhou Huqingyutang Pharmaceutical Co., Ltd. and Hangzhou Zhiweiguan Co., Ltd., Centennial Huichang was set up in 1800, with the original name of "Huichang South-North Store." In the Daoguang period of the Qing Dynasty, the preserved fruit and candles produced by it were selected to be tributes; in the Guangxu period of the Qing Dynasty, "Huichang" was designated as the supplier for the Imperial Household Department; in West Lake Expo 1929, sweet-scented osmanthus ginger and other preserved fruits of "Huichang" won the special award, the highest award at that time.

The "Centennial Huichang" store now stands at the crossroads of Shuibei Street and West Shitang Street. An aunt sitting by the door is making rice dumplings. Only a glance at their meat stuffing and bamboo leaves reveals the superlarge size of a finished product that is enough to eat an ordinary people's fill by just a single one. Cakes and pastries, preserved fruit, and loquat flowers are all displayed in sample and old packages in the store. Looking inside, you will see four characters of "Tangxi Guild Hall" framed on the wall, under which is the plaque writing "Tangxi Town Yu Ming Theoretical Propaganda Studio." Mr.Yu is the person in charge of this store, and he is a local 'storyteller' with a very kind look.

I asked a few more questions. By lucky coincidence, there were not many customers in the store so Mr. Yu made a pot of tea and started to tell me stories of Tangxi. In early times, blessed with the Beijing-Hangzhou Grand Canal, Tangxi attracted merchants from far and wide who settled down here and dominated their own industry. Huizhou people were at the top of "the food chain," setting up pawnshops. Besides, Ningbo people made cakes and pastries, Cixi people produced medicine, people from Danyang, Jiangsu sold flour, Shaoxing people brewed alcohol, and Dongyang people were plasterers. Mr.Yu talked about the experience of his ancestors leaving Ningbo to make a living in Tangxi, the personnel changes of two time-honored brands of Centennial Huichang and Wengchangchun, and the ups and downs of the wealthy in Tangxi Town, and showed me his precious collection of cake and pastry molds in the end. After that, I couldn't help feeling that the hour of sharing was filled with the joy and sorrow in the world and the rise and fall of life. Things are like flowers and grass always existing in spring, while humans are like floating clouds dissipating without even a shadow left. We as humans should make more pragmatic effort to better benefit the world.

梅干
Dried Plums

话梅
Refined Plum

梅肉
Refined Plum(seedless)

　　水北一片不大，若是走马观花，一个小时足够了，但若是细细品味，也能让人心甘情愿消磨一下午。逛到水北街西端，人流渐少，清静中见到两层小楼的临平方志馆，新布置的互动展陈让人毫不费力走近临平的来龙去脉。作为展示临平文化特质与形象的重要窗口，塘栖古镇上还有运河文化遗产展示厅、塘栖书院、皮影戏非遗馆等文化场馆，让游客在休闲逛吃之余，也能放慢脚步、驻足品读，在场馆中穿越时光与历史对话，重回货船云集、仓库林立、挑夫卸货号声此起彼伏的黄金水岸。

The Shuibei area is not large. As a cursory trip there needs only an hour, a whole afternoon spent there will allow you to savor each step of the journey as you want. Along the west end of Shuibei Street, visitors are fewer. The two-storied Linping Local Chronicles Museum standing quietly shows the historical development of Linping to visitors easily with newly installed interactive exhibitions. As a major window to demonstrate the culture and image of Linping, Linping Ancient Town is also equipped with Canal Cultural Heritage Exhibition Hall, Tangxi Academy, Chinese Shadow Puppetry Intangible Cultural Heritage Museum, and other cultural venues. In doing so, besides relaxing, going shopping, and enjoying food, tourists can also slow down to "read." They engage in conversations with history by traveling through time in venues, and get back to the golden banks by which cargo ships are gathering, warehouses are standing in great numbers, and porters are unloading and shouting slogans one after another.

沿广济桥这条中轴线向南延伸，穿过古镇标志性的三开仪门石牌坊继续向南，不远处的绿色水荡间，坐落着浙江塘栖盲人门球基地。2023 年 10 月，这里将作为 2022 杭州亚残运会承办盲人门球的比赛场地。

盲人门球运动，需要运动员根据触觉来确定自己在场上的位置；球内有铃铛，球滚动时会发出声音，运动员根据听觉来判断球的方向和速度。水荡环绕，形成天然屏障，为这项盲人运动提供了绝佳的安静场地。

Exploring southwards along the axis of Guangji Bridge through the signature three-door stone archway, you will see the Zhejiang Tangxi Goalball Base sitting by the green lake. In October 2023, the goalball competition of the 4th Asian Para Games Hangzhou 2022 will be held right here.

While playing goalball, blind athletes need to spot their locations through the sense of touch, and judge the direction and speed of the goalball through the sense of hearing as the bell inside will ring when the goalball is rolling. The surrounding water shapes a natural barrier, giving goalball players an ideally quiet venue to play.

盲人门球
Goalball

我小时候关于塘栖的记忆，只有三样东西——黄澄澄的枇杷、紫红色的荸荠、青光泛起的甘蔗，吃起来都挺麻烦。荸荠生吃最好，但是小小的扁圆，去皮相当烦琐，刀法讲究，我们小孩子一般只能边啃皮边吐皮，纵然麻烦，也舍不得那口清甜新鲜；后来看书上写鲁迅先生喜欢冬天风干后的荸荠，因为失去水分后更甜，我暗自担心果皮皱得像葡萄干似的怎样才能去掉。甘蔗的食用程序，在古镇上已经得到了升级，省却了削皮、切段、吐渣的麻烦，榨成甘蔗汁，插上吸管捧在手里边走边喝，清凉又方便。枇杷的食用，丰子恺先生在他的散文《塘栖》里这样描述："在船里吃枇杷是一件快适的事。吃枇杷要剥皮，要出核，把手弄脏，把桌子弄脏。吃好之后必须收拾桌子，洗手，实在麻烦。船里吃枇杷就没有这种麻烦。靠在船窗口吃，皮和核都丢在河里，吃好之后在河里洗手。"确实，要吃到一口新鲜的枇杷，果子剥了皮还要去籽去蒂，边吃边汁水滴答，果汁滴到的地方黏黏发黄，吃起来总是有些烦琐狼狈。我每每躲在家里大吃一通枇杷，吃得指甲缝里蜡黄，好几天才褪去。

There are only three things in my memory about Tangxi, namely yellow loquat, burgundy water chestnuts, and green sugarcane, which are all not convenient to eat. It is best to eat water chestnuts raw, but they are small and oblate, which requires skillful cutting to remove the shell. Then kids like us had no choice but to peel it with our mouth, reluctant to give up the freshness and sweetness. Later, reading that Mr. Lu Xun loves the air-dried water chestnuts in winter for a sweeter taste after drying out, I started to fret about how to remove the shell as wrinkled as raisins. As for sugarcane, local people have upgraded the way to eat it, streamlining the troublesome process of peeling, cutting, and residue spitting into the only step of juice squeezing. It is cool and convenient to drink the sugarcane juice through a straw while walking. When it comes to loquat, as Mr. Feng Zikai described in his prose Tangxi, "It's quite pleasant to eat loquat on a boat. To eat loquat, you need to remove the peel and spit the pits, which makes your hands and table dirty. After eating, you have to wash your hands and tidy up the table, which is indeed troublesome. But it is not so inconvenient if you eat on the boat. Sitting by the window, you can throw the peel and pits into the river and wash your hands in the river after you finish." Exactly, to have a bite of a fresh loquat, you have to remove peel, stalk, and pit and bear the dripping juice. Things with juice drips will become sticky and yellow, which makes it kind of tricky and embarrassing to eat. Every time I stay at home to engorge loquat it will make my fingernails' cracks as yellow as wax, which always doesn't fade for days.

甘蔗汁
Sugarcane Juice

枇杷
Loquat

荸荠
Water Chestnuts

塘栖枇杷起于隋唐，流传至今已有千余年的历史厚度。关于塘栖枇杷的故事，都收藏在塘栖枇杷产业博览馆里。这个展馆就在塘栖古镇入口处，围绕圆圆的小枇杷，沉浸式展陈布置得相当惊艳。

如果不执着于枇杷作为水果的原汁原味，那枇杷也是可以便利食用的，比如塘栖的枇杷膏，还有塘栖老字号企业同福永酒厂推出了甜甜的枇杷果酒。同福永也是百年老字号品牌，可追溯到清末光绪年间，他家的白酒被当地老百姓亲切地称为"塘茅"（塘栖茅台）。

枇杷酒
Loquat Fruit Wine

Originated in Sui and Tang Dynasties, Tangxi loquat has gone through thousands of years. As for stories of Tangxi loquat, they are all collected in the Tangxi Loquat Industry Museum. At the entrance of the Tangxi Ancient Town stands the museum surrounded by small, round loquats, which enjoys amazingly immersive arrangement.

If the loquat is not eaten for its original taste and flavor as fruit, it can be consumed as processed food, such as the Loquat Leaf Extract of Tangxi, and the Loquat Fruit Wine produced by time-honored Hangzhou Tongfuyong Wine Co., Ltd. As a century-old brand, the origin of Tongfuyong dates back to the Guangxu period of the late Qing Dynasty, and its white liquor is nicknamed "Tangmao"(Moutai of Tangxi) by local citizens.

如今枇杷已是多地的重要产业，塘栖之外，南方的枇杷早早上市，个头挺大，还水嫩光滑，但我觉得滋味远不如塘栖5月底长了"斑"的小枇杷鲜甜。产地多了，对产品加以区别保护很有必要。塘栖的枇杷不负众望地获得了中国国家农产品地理标志登记保护。为了擦亮这张"金名片"，塘栖每年5月下旬举行枇杷采摘节。来采枇杷、买枇杷的人多了，塘栖开始考虑围绕枇杷产业链来打造未来乡村。比如塘栖村，一路行过，家家户户门前院后都种着枇杷树，树不高，青绿的叶子又密又大，以野蛮的生命力点染着蜿蜒的村中小路。村里以打造"中国枇杷第一村"为目标，投入大手笔，对村庄环境和基础配套设施进行了完善提升。经过改造的塘栖村成了典型的江南乡村，粉墙黛瓦、家家庭院，像吴冠中笔下的水墨画一样别致又明快。

The loquat industry has already evolved into one of the major industries in multiple places. Outside Tangxi, some loquats have already come into season in the south, being in large size, juicy and smooth. But I hold that the taste is far from satisfactory while compared with the small and spotted ones turning ripe in May in Tangxi. As places of origin increase, it becomes extremely necessary to distinguish and protect different varieties. As expected, the Tangxi loquat becomes one of the products protected and registered by Agro-product Geographical Indications of the PRC. To polish the gold business card, Tangxi holds the Loquat Picking Festival every last third of May. As more people come to pick and buy loquat, Tangxi starts to build itself into a future village with the loquat industry at the center. Take Tangxi Village as an example, each household there plants loquat trees at the front door and back yard. Though not tall, the loquat trees grow thick and large leaves, decorating the winding paths in the village with wild vitality. To build the "Top Village of Loquat in China," local people have made great investments and improved the environment and infrastructure there. After renovation, Tangxi Village has turned into a model of Jiangnan villages. White walls and black tiles and the yard of each household are as unique and bright as the ink-wash paintings of Wu Guanzhong.

枇杷烧肉
Red-braised Pork Belly with Loquat

红烧羊肉
Stewed Mutton

粢毛肉圆
Glutinous-Rice Meatballs

细沙羊尾
Red Bean Paste Sticky Rice Ball

环境变好了，来的人更多了，乡村旅游配套得跟上，农家乐一家家开起来。塘栖的饮食，江南水乡的精致与运河船家的质朴汇聚一堂，用料讲究的塘栖板鸭、滑嫩爽脆的油爆河虾、米粒晶莹的粢毛肉圆、香甜诱人的细沙羊尾……传统的塘栖美食为乡村带来了更多收入。除了枇杷采摘活动，塘栖村还为来客提供了大草坪露营地、卡丁车俱乐部、生态体验园、水上游线等项目，一幅农业农村与时俱进的美好蓝图在这里铺呈开来。

As the environment improves, tourists increase. Then, facilities supporting rural tourism follow and local catering and home-stay industries start to flourish. The food of Tangxi, the elegance of the Jiangnan village, and boatmen living plainly all gather here. Traditional delicacies of Tangxi, including high-quality Tangxi Dried Salted Duck, tender and crisp Sauteed River Prawns, crystal Glutinous-Rice Meatballs, as well as attractive and sweet Red Bean Paste Sticky Rice Ball are generating higher revenue for the village. Besides loquat picking, Tangxi Village also provides tourists with a great lawn for camping, a karting club, an ecological park, water cruises and so on, drawing a beautiful blueprint featuring the agriculture and rural area advancing with the times.

枇杷馆的隔壁，一幢民国气质的两层青砖小楼安静又谦逊地立于路边。这就是何思敬纪念馆，由何氏故居改建而来。何先生 1896 生于塘栖，1932 年加入中国共产党，是《中国人民政治协商会议共同纲领》和新中国首部宪法的起草人之一，被誉为"法学泰斗"，被毛泽东称赞为"全国第一流的法学家"。何先生怀着他那一代党员知识分子的纯粹与忠诚，凭自己的学识参与了我党从抗日到重庆谈判，到建国立宪，再到普法教育的各个阶段，用生命践行了光明磊落、正直的品质和为党奋斗的信念，在古镇上撑起一片正能量的红色天空。

Next to the Loquat Museum stands a two-storied brick building, quietly and honestly featuring the architectural style of the Republic of China by the road. It is the He Sijing Memorial Hall reconstructed from Mr. He's former residence. Born in 1896 in Tangxi and becoming a member of the Communist Party of China in 1932, Mr. He was one of the drafters of the Common Program of the CPPCC and the first constitution of the PRC, thus praised as "a law authority" and "national first-class jurist" by Mao Zedong. With the pureness and loyalty of intellectual CPC members in his generation, Mr.He gave full play to his knowledge to participate in various events of our Party from the Anti-Japanese War to Chongqing Negotiations, to the founding of the PRC and establishment of the constitution, and to law popularization, practiced the virtues of openness and transparency, integrity, and hard work for the Party, and shored up a red sky of positive energy in the ancient town.

何思敬
Mr. He Sijing

The Spirit of Yalan Village Passes Down Over

鸭兰薪火代代相传

塘栖古镇的附近，还有另一个关于永恒信仰的红色故事在闪闪发光。位于崇贤街道的鸭兰村，是杭州市第一个党支部的诞生地。1927年四一二反革命政变后，革命处于低潮期，中共杭州地委转移工作重点，积极开辟农村革命阵地，同年6月，中共鸭兰村支部应运而生、知难而进。如今这里建立起中共鸭兰村支部旧址陈列馆，记录了鸭兰村那段赴汤蹈火的革命往事，亦梳理了薪火相传的当代发展。站在这个红色起点，开启一场重温初心、洗礼精神的问心之旅，用先烈的无畏气概为自己的梦想加油鼓劲。

Near the Tangxi Ancient Town, there is another shining red story about eternal belief. The Yalan village in Chongxian Subdistrict is the birthplace of Hangzhou's first Party branch. After the counter-revolutionary coup on April 12th, 1927, the revolution was at a low ebb and the Regional CPC Committee of Hangzhou shifted the focus of work to explore a base for rural revolution. In June of the same year, the Yalan Party Branch was born as the fruit of efforts to advance despite difficulties. Nowadays, an exhibition hall has been built here to memorize the revolution of Yalan village through fire and water and the development in modern times through generations. Let's stand at such a red starting point to embark on a journey to review original missions and get baptized spiritually, and cheer ourselves up with martyrs' fearlessness to pursue our dreams.

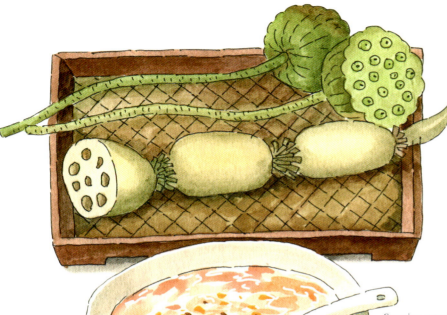

走出陈列馆，边上就是村里的文化礼堂。礼堂中陈列着崇贤街道的特产——藕粉。崇贤藕粉曾拥有作为国礼的高光时刻：1972年美国总统尼克松访华，在杭州品尝到一味特殊的美食，它看起来是淡淡的粉褐色，如布丁一般晶莹润弹，一入口，比布丁更为细腻柔软，还带着自然的清甜。总统先生对这种新奇的东方食品赞不绝口，周总理亲自挑选了以崇贤三家村藕为原料制成的藕粉，作为国礼让总统先生带回大洋彼岸。周到细致的总理对三家村藕粉的信赖是有产业历史支撑的。三家村藕粉作为贡品，自南宋一直延续至清朝。清《唐栖志》在"藕粉"词条下这样记载："藕粉者，屑藕汁之，他处多伪，掺真膺各半，唯唐栖三家村业此者以藕贱不必假他物为之也。"真是有趣，因为藕贱而制作出原汁原味的纯真藕粉、绝无掺假，三家村人一如本地藕粉般无添加地天真淳朴。

2016年，三家村手削藕粉制作技艺被列为浙江省非物质文化遗产代表性项目名录。注意，手削藕粉的成品藕粉是片状的，并不是普通的颗粒或粉末状。

三家村藕粉
Sanjia Village Lotus Root Starch

Stepping out of the exhibition hall, you will see the cultural hall of the village, which displays the lotus root starch, a special local product of Chongxian Subdistrict. Chongxian Lotus Root Starch once enjoyed the highlight as the state gift. When American President Nixon visited China in 1972, he tasted a special delicacy in Hangzhou which was pink-brown and as crystal and springy as pudding. Having a taste, you would find it not only softer than pudding but also naturally fresh and sweet. President Nixon was full of praise for such a fantastic oriental delicacy; therefore Premier Zhou Enlai selected the lotus root starch made of the lotus root grown in Sanjia Village of Chongxian as the state gift for President Nixon to bring back to America. Considerate Premier Zhou's trust in Sanjia Village Lotus Root Starch is supported by its industrial history. Sanjia Village Lotus Root Starch has been designated as a tribute from the Southern Song Dynasty to Qing Dynasty. As recorded in the *Records of Tangxi* in the Qing Dynasty, "Lotus root starch is made of the sediment from the sap of mashed lotus root. There are many shoddy products being half-genuine and half-sham. Only Sanjia Village in Tangxi Town produces it 100% with lotus root." It is quite interesting that the lotus root starch reserves its original taste and flavor by only using lotus root as its raw material with the simple reason of low cost originally. Local people of Sanjia Village are also as simple as local additive-free Lotus Root Starch.

In 2016, Sanjia Village lotus root hand-slicing technology was listed as a representative project of the intangible cultural heritage of Zhejiang. It is worth noting that sliced lotus root starch is in the shape of slices, rather than common particles or powder.

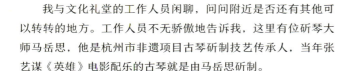

我与文化礼堂的工作人员闲聊，问问附近是否还有其他可以转转的地方。工作人员不无骄傲地告诉我，这里有位斫琴大师马岳思，他是杭州市非遗项目古琴斫制技艺传承人，当年张艺谋《英雄》电影配乐的古琴就是由马岳思斫制。

I chatted with a staff member of the cultural hall to find out if there are any other places nearby to visit. She was very proud to tell me that Ma Yuesi, a master of "Zhuoqin," or Guqin making, is an inheritor of Hangzhou's intangible cultural heritage of Guqin-making technique. The soundtrack of Zhang Yimou's movie *Hero* was produced exactly by the Guqin made by Mr. Ma.

斫琴
Zhuoqin

制作古琴的技艺则被雅称为"斫琴"，是一门融合音乐、造型、漆艺为一体的工艺，被列为杭州市非物质文化遗产。善弹者善斫，斫琴传人也是善于抚琴、听琴之人。

The fine technique of making Guqin has an elegant name called "Zhuoqin," which is a craft integrating the music, model and lacquer art and is listed as one of Hangzhou's intangible cultural heritages. Those who are good at playing Guqin are good at Guqin-making as well, and the descendants of Guqin makers are also good Guqin players and listeners.

毗邻都市繁华，坐拥山水生态，崇贤与塘栖的生态文化资源优势，使其成为临平对接杭州城西科创大走廊的桥头堡，更成为高水平建设临平大运河国家文化公园（大运河科创城）的十足底气。大运河科创城是临平着力构建发展新动力的平台，以塘栖古镇为建设的核心区，以文创、科创双策源驱动。在大运河畔的湖山肌理间，悉心植入科创、文创等技术含量高、创新能力强的产业功能，既保护运河的大环境、围绕遗产恢复历史意象，又能持续对运河文化事项进行挖掘提炼与研究普及，持续活化遗产，还能为临平发展打造全新的产业高地，可谓一举而多赢，颇具智慧。在这个全新的平台上，已引进清大文产杭州数字研究院、锐健医疗股份有限公司、浙江菲尔特过滤科技股份有限公司等重大产业项目，运河边的新梦，已草蛇灰线，初具雏形。

Sitting next to prosperous cities and surrounded by mountains and waters, Chongxian and Tangxi enjoy the ecological and cultural advantages to develop into bridgeheads for Linping to connect Hangzhou West Science and Technology Innovation Corridor, and to lay foundations for the construction of the Grand Canal (Linping section) National Cultural Park & the Grand Canal (Linping section) Science and Technology Innovation City. With Tangxi Ancient Town at the center, the Grand Canal (Linping section) Science and Technology Innovation City is a platform driven by dual forces of scientific and cultural innovation for Linping to generate new development impetus. Integrating scientific and cultural innovation industries and other high-tech and innovative industries into the Grand Canal area, people not only can protect the environment of the Grand Canal and revive historical images of heritages, but also continue to extract, study and popularize canal culture, as well as creating brand-new highland for the development of Linping. It is wisdom of achieving many things at one stroke. Many major industrial programs including Tsingta Culture Industry Planning Design and Research Institute (Hangzhou), Hangzhou Rejoin Medical Co., Ltd., and Zhejiang Filter Technology Co., Ltd. have already settled down on this new stage. The new dream by the Canal is taking shape.

XPLORING THE COUNTRYSI
ISCOVERING A BEAUTIFUL
ENERY BY THE CANAL BAN

细嗅乡野，河畔花开

一座城繁华的背面，是张弛有度、作息有节。运河与城市相伴相生，城里人孜孜以求的吾心安处，恰是大运河畔如珍珠般散落的小小村庄。它们正以田间地头酝酿萌动的点点变幻，诠释着沧海桑田、人间共富。

Behind the bustling city lies a rhythm of leisure and regular routine. Where the city meets the Canal in harmonious coexistence, the serenity sought by urban dwellers is found in the humble villages, scattered like pearls along the Grand Canal. All the subtle changes in the fields give expression to the reshaping of the area and the realization of common prosperity.

从塘栖古镇八字桥出发，一路向南，有一条定制的观景道——塘超小径，全长约 20 千米，途经田园、树林、村庄、小桥、湿地，小径的尽头，是拔地而起的超山。

超山是临平境内最北、最有名的山。"十里梅花香雪海"，说的就是一夜春风催花开后，十余里海如彩云绕山的超山胜景。但梅海如雪只是超山梅花闻名天下的原因之一。其二，超山梅古。我国有楚、晋、隋、唐、宋五大古梅，超山有唐梅、宋梅，一山独占二株，而且都会开花，其中唐梅开出的花还是非常珍贵的六瓣白梅。再看其三，那就是海派金石大家、西泠印社首任社长吴昌硕对超山梅花的文化加持。"十年不到香雪海，梅花忆我我忆梅。"吴老先生太爱超山的梅花了，尤其喜欢枝干虬劲的宋梅；自己来超山还不够，多次带着朋友、学生等文化圈名人后辈来超山吟诗作画刻印，在这里留下穿越时空的宝贵财富。最后的最后，吴昌硕老先生把自己永远留在了超山——这里有老先生的墓，还建起了吴昌硕纪念馆。

超山风景区挺大，有 5 平方千米，每年 1 月到 3 月都是赏梅期。花飞满天的时节，这里必定游人如织，热闹非常，如今叠加上露营风潮、小商小贩，在超山赏梅竟然有了赏樱的错觉。

梅花在中国文化里奋勇当先、凌寒独放的形象，何以在超山突变为大众娱乐？这跟运河兴盛了塘栖的蜜饯产业有很大关系。塘栖很早就产水果，但因为水果运输不便、难以保存，大都自产自销，并没有形成特别的产业。这样的情况被明代一个叫吕需的人改变了。根据光绪《唐栖志》记载，外地人吕需将外地的蜜饯制作技艺传入塘栖。从此以后，水果运输和保存的问题都得到了解决，塘栖人卖蜜饯的生意就开始了。春天，他们在超山种植大片梅花，夏天，采梅子做成蜜饯，走水路运出去，蜜饯随运河流波成为塘栖特产发扬光大，而超山的梅花也因此愈发漫山遍野、长盛不衰。

唐梅
The Tang Plum

唐梅

Emerging from the Bazi Bridge in Tangxi Ancient Town, a bespoke scenic trail, the Tangchao Trail, goes towards the south. Stretching approximately 20 kilometers, it meanders through pastures, woods, villages, bridges, and wetlands and Chaoshan Mountain ascends at the end of trail.

Chaoshan Mountain, the northernmost and most famous peak in Linping, is renowned for its "ten-li fragrant sea of plum blossoms." This poetic depiction speaks of the spectacle when a spring breeze coaxes the flowers into bloom, creating a sea of blossoms that shroud the mountain in vibrant, cloud-like formations for more than ten li. Yet, this snow-like ocean of plums represents merely one facet of the global fame Chaoshan Mountain's plum blossoms enjoy. The historical lineage of Chaoshan Mountain's plums is another attraction. Secondly, throughout history, our nation has cherished five ancient plums, which hail from the Chu state and the Jin, Sui, Tang, and Song Dynasties, with the Tang and Song plums gracing Chaoshan Mountain. On this mountain, two types of plums flourish, including the rare six-petaled white plums of the Tang Dynasty. Thirdly, the cultural endorsement of Chaoshan Mountain's plum blossoms by Wu Changshuo, the inaugural president of the Xiling Seal Engraver's Society, is indispensable. He passionately penned, "Haven't been to the Fragrant Snow Sea for ten years, plum blossoms remember me, and I remember plum." His affection for the sturdy-branched Song plum was profound. He would also bring along friends, students, and other luminaries from the cultural sphere to render artistic tributes to Chaoshan Mountain, thus gifting it a timeless treasure of poetry, paintings and seals. In the end, Wu Changshuo immortalized himself on Chaoshan

Mountain — the mountain cradles the final resting place of the old artist, and also stands as the site for the Wu Changshuo Memorial Hall.

The expansive Chaoshan Mountain Scenic Area, spanning 5 square kilometers, offers a canvas for plum viewing from January to March each year. In this season, with flowers pedals flying in the breeze, the area would be filled with visitors. The trend of camping, together with small traders and street vendors, make the Chaoshan Mountain plum spectacle seem like cherry blossom viewing.

How did the image of plum blossoms, a representative of vanguard blossoming against cold in Chinese culture, transform into public entertainment at Chaoshan Mountain? It tied to the flourishing preserved fruit industry in Tangxi, located by the canal. Tangxi had been a fruit-producing area for a long time, yet the difficulty of transporting and preserving fruits meant that most were consumed locally, failing to cultivate a distinct industry. However, this was changed by Lü Xu in the Ming Dynasty. As recorded in the Guangxu period of *Records of Tangxi*, Lü Xu introduced the art of preserved fruit production to Tangxi from elsewhere. This innovation provided a solution to the challenges of fruit transportation and preservation, paving the way for Tangxi locals to start a thriving business selling preserved fruits. In spring, vast plum blossoms would bloom in Chaoshan Mountain. When summer comes, these plums would be harvested to produce candied fruits, transported outward via waterways. As the Canal currents carried the preserves far and wide, they became Tangxi's signature product. Consequently, the plum blossoms flourished here, their abundance and prosperity ever-increasing.

宋梅
The Song Plum

吴昌硕
Wu Changshuo

塘超小径

Tangchao Trail

与超山风光交相辉映的，是塘栖镇南部的丁山湖。丁山湖是一个原生态湿地，一个容你坐船游湖、观光垂钓的休闲度假之地。如果走塘超小径，你一定会遇见让你一见难忘的丁山湖，它是临平乡村风景的后起之秀，难得的乡村宝藏。

丁山湖段塘超小径弯弯曲曲地盘桓在原生态湿地上，部分是凌驾水上的木栈道，部分是普通河堤上的滨水步道，时不时点缀着轩榭廊坊等江南建筑，步道两侧则是杨柳依依、芦苇丛生的湿地景象。春天的丁山湖仿佛打翻了艺术家的调色盘，美得出乎意料，我一去再去。走上栈道，湖上清风扑面、碧波潋滟，身边桃红梨白，郁金香成片；栈道路口，有当地老人摆地摊卖着特色农产品，荸荠、茨菰、马兰头、螺蛳、自家产的土鸡蛋，新鲜又生态；栈道上凭栏眺望，普贤菩萨骑着六牙神象屹立水中，远处蓝天下，白鹭翩飞，丁河村的经典杭派民居排布得整整齐齐。

来城郊度假的人，着实需要一条这样水润清灵的栈道，让紧张的自己恢复松弛、蓄满元气。游步道两侧的栅栏上，绿植显得干净而光洁，每隔一定距离都会出现一个白色搪瓷杯。我打开两个杯盖，里面什么也没有，开到第三个杯盖，里面有两个烟蒂，哦，原来是隐藏式垃圾桶！算是个出乎意料的贴心细节设计。挨着湖的农家乐与民宿，一家挨着一家，景色和食物都不错，本地水产做得尤其鲜嫩，而且价格公道。恰好的天气，找个恰好的亲水平台景观位坐下，任风从湖上来，与我擦肩而过，把一众游客高高低低的笑声传到村庄。

Complementing Chaoshan Mountain is Dingshan Lake, nestled in the southern parts of Tangxi Town. As an untouched ecological wetland, Dingshan Lake serves as a getaway for leisure and vacation, inviting you to explore its waters by boat, sightseeing, or fishing. Travelers along the Tangchao Trail will meet this unforgettably tranquil body of water. As an emerging gem in Linping's pastoral scenery, Dingshan Lake is indeed a rare rural treasure.

The Dingshan Lake section of the Tangchao Trail meanders through the wetland. Portions of it rise above the water as wooden boardwalks, while others trace the banks as typical waterfront paths, punctuated by characteristic Jiangnan structures such as a gazebo, over-water pavilion, colonnade and boat-shaped waterfront building. Flanking the trail is a symphony of willows and reeds. In spring, Dingshan Lake appears as if an artist's palette had overturned, presenting a riot of colors in an unexpected display of beauty. It is a sight that calls for a return. As one strolls along the boardwalk, the lake's breeze is gentle,

its waters shimmering in blue, white clusters of peach and pear blossoms dotting the view, and patches of tulips enlivening the scene. At intersections along the boardwalk, local elders vend their special agricultural produce: water chestnuts, arrowheads, local potherbs called Malantou, river snails, and home-laid eggs, all fresh and ecologically sourced. From the boardwalk's railing, the statue of Samantabhadra Bodhisattva can be seen standing serenely upon a six-tusked elephant, submerged in the water. In the distance, under the blue sky, egrets take flight, and classic Hangzhou-style dwellings of Dinghe Village line up in orderly harmony.

Such a pristine boardwalk beside water is precise to those travel to the suburb seeking refreshing change and energy after hectic life. The fences along the hiking trail are adorned with vibrant green plants, gleaming in their freshness, interrupted at regular intervals by white enamel cups. Upon opening two of the cup lids, I find

them empty. However, the third reveals two discarded cigarette butts. Ah, an ingeniously concealed trash receptacle! Such an unexpected, yet thoughtful design detail. Farmhouses and home-stays are near the lake, each offering appealing vistas and delectable meals. The local aquatic produce is particularly fresh and tender, priced reasonably. When the weather is suitable, you can sit down at a perfect lakeside viewing spot where you can feel the wind breezing past you, carrying the laughters of fellow visitors into the surrounding villages.

丁山湖
Dingshan Lake

Happy
幸福的院子
Yard

　　丁山湖畔的村庄，受惠于湿地、塘超小径的闲适风光，并紧紧抓住了风光带来的机遇。丁河村成了共同富裕示范点、未来乡村的样板村。村里打造的鱼鹰团供应链，通过线上线下销售相结合、团体个人采购相结合的方式，拓宽了当地粽子、粢毛肉圆、糕团、板鸭、蔬菜等诸多产品的销售渠道。打开天猫超市、京东、抖音、拼多多等平台，搜索"丁山河"，下单，你就能尝到临平的乡村好味道。

　　再看隔壁的丁山河村，深谙"乡愁"流量密码，用活的"老底子"手艺来为本地特产销售赋能引流。丁山河村本身是一个典型的古运河畔"手艺村"，村里保留着两家百年老字号、一项世界级非遗项目"清水丝绵"、五项省市区级非遗项目。如何保护好、传承好、利用好这些文化遗产，助力乡村振兴、共同富裕呢？村里的老刀食品有自己的新思路。老刀出资将村里的废弃小学改造成非遗体验基地——百匠工坊（幸福的院子），在工坊院子里搭建起老虎灶、回龙灶、缸缸灶等传统美食生产设备；更新了场景后，老刀再邀请村里 30 多位老手艺人"重出江湖"，挖掘、恢复生产传统食品。这几年下来，老刀的百匠工坊让土灶月饼、麻酥糖、草木灰咸鸭蛋、米塑技艺等 56 个品种的传统食品重新出现在大家的生活里。每到节假日前夕，百匠工坊的老师傅们总是忙得应接不暇，季节限定的特产，出道即是巅峰、出炉即成爆款，产品联接 100 多家农户，为村里的手艺人直接增加收入 100 多万元。这份由文化非遗到物质共富的答卷交得真漂亮！

Villages situated along Dingshan Lake reap the benefits of their picturesque wetland and canal settings, seizing the opportunities presented by the breathtaking scenery. Dinghe Village has emerged as a pilot of common prosperity and a sample for future village development. The establishment of the Yuyingtuan group purchase supply chain within the village has significantly widened sales channels for local products. Rice dumplings, meatballs, rice cakes, dried salted ducks, vegetables, and an array of other items now enjoy expanded market access through online and offline sales and both group and individual procurement strategies. When you simply open platforms like Tmall Supermarket, JD.COM, TikTok, Pinduoduo, and others, search for "Dingshan River," place an order, and you're on the way to savoring the delightful tastes of Linping's countryside.

Dingshanhe Village, situated nearby, has a profound understanding of the intrinsic value of "homesickness" and employs the time-honored craft of the "old foundation" to drive the sales of local specialties. The village is itself a "craft village" along the ancient canal, boasting two century-old brands, one of which is recognized as a world-class intangible cultural heritage known as "Rinsing Silk Wadding." Additionally, the village is home to five provincial-, municipal- and autonomously regional intangible cultural heritage projects. The question arises of how to protect, preserve and effectively utilize these cultural heritages to contribute to rural revitalization and common prosperity. Laodao Food in the village has devised innovative approaches. Laodao has generously funded the transformation of the abandoned village primary school into a non-legacy experiential base called Baijiang Workshop (Happy Yard). Traditional food production equipment, such as a tiger stove, recycling cooking bench, and cylinder stove, have been installed in the workshop yard. By reviving the traditional food production, Laodao has invited over 30

米塑立夏狗
Rice Sculpture Dog (a kind of traditional snack for summer begins)

veteran artists from the village to "make a reappearance after years of retirement," rekindling the production of traditional delicacies. Over the years, Baijiang Workshop, under the guidance of Laodao, has reintroduced 56 varieties of traditional foods, including earthen stove moon cakes, crisp candies, salted duck eggs with plant ash, and rice sculpture skills, into the lives of people. On the eve of holidays, the master craftsmen of Baijiang Workshop are always overwhelmed with orders. Their limited-season special products create a sensation upon release, generating significant demand. These products have forged connections with over 100 farmer households, directly increasing the income of village artisans by more than RMB 1 million. This transformation, from cultural heritage to material wealth, paints a truly beautiful picture of success!

　　塘栖的传统糕点产业也挺"卷"的，每种产品质量都很挺好，渠道搭建也都差不多，老刀只能另辟蹊径，通过季节限定、传统手工与沉浸式制作体验让产品古今相映、脱颖而出。

The traditional pastry industry in Tangxi is in fierce competition. Each product enjoys high quality, and the channels of distribution are also similar. However, Laodao has charted a different path. By embracing seasonal suppiles, fostering a traditional and hands-on production experience, the products echo the old tradition and new fashion, ultimately standing out from the rest.

喜欢来运河边健步走的人，为沿运河走路这件事起了个好听的名字——"走运"。

People who take pleasure in strolling along the canal delightfully call it "zouyun" (which means walking along the canal, the same pronunciation as have good luck).

大运河畔的村庄，在崇贤、塘栖、超山一带，是河网如织、碧波清流的样态；随着河水东去，到了临平东北的运河街道，延续成另一番绿野相拥的美丽景象。这番变化，沿着以大运河杭州塘为主轴的 29 千米生态廊道渐次发生。其中，绿道的五杭集镇东明路段尤为让我印象深刻：运河两岸绝没有拂堤杨柳的醉态，却植了两排高大笔直的粗壮香樟树，使这段河道显得尤为镇静穆然、气宇不凡。

The villages along the Grand Canal, in the Chongxian, Tangxi, and Chaoshan Mountain area, are characterized by interconnected river networks and crystal-clear blue waves. As the river flows eastward, it converges with the Yunhe Subdistrict in the northeastern part of Linping, unfolding another image of verdant fields embracing one another. This transition gradually occurs along the 29-kilometer ecological corridor, with Hangzhou section serving as its center. Among these scenic wonders, the Dongming Road in Wuhang market town left a lasting impression on me. Here, the riverbanks are not adorned with swaying willows that evoke a sense of intoxication. Instead, two rows of tall, straight, and robust camphor trees take their place. This stretch of the river shows a sense of tranquility, which give rises to an extraordinary atmosphere.

东明路绿道
Dongming Greenway

运河边的文创园里，一砖一石，涛声人语。

In the Creative Park near the canal, bricks and stones whisper tales, and the gentle lapping of waves resembles the sound of voices.

绿道旁，你一定不会错过一座高高的水塔。当一座城市轰轰烈烈地往前跑、生机勃勃地大放异彩时，水塔下的光阴却走得慢了些。这里就是 20 世纪 80 年代曾经盛极一时的浙江麻纺厂余杭分厂（当时临平是余杭县府所在地）。毗邻运河五杭段，当时享有河海之利，但最终大浪淘沙地成了时代的眼泪。时光随手一提，都是不舍的青春，幸好大运河科创城赋予了这片园区新生。老厂房经过空间重塑、功能再造，惊艳转型为新地标——大运河 1986 文创园，每一步都踏出工业时代与时尚产业的粘连。园区独具特色的波浪形红砖外墙，成为绿道掩映下的醒目风景；曾经以实用为先的冰冷水塔，开辟出了引领园区嗅觉的东塔咖啡；麻纺厂职工商店、齿轮与女工雕塑，仍铭记着曾经的工业遗风。

大运河 1986 文创园

Beside the greenway, an unmissable sight awaits—a towering water tower. As the city propels forward with vigor, time seems to slow down beneath the water tower. This is the Yuhang Branch of Zhejiang Hemp Mill, once thriving in the 1980s. Situated adjacent to the Wuhang section of the canal, it once enjoyed the advantages bestowed by water courses and seas. However, in the end, the tides of change washed away sand, leaving behind the tears of bygone times. When past is mentioned, it speaks not of youth. Fortunately, the Grand Canal Science and Technology Innovation City has breathed new life into this park. Through spatial and functional reconstruction of the old factory buildings, a new landmark has emerged—the Grand Canal 1986 Creative Park, a combination of the industrial era and the fashion industry. The park's distinctive wavy red brick exterior wall has become a captivating sight in the green-way's shade. The once utilitarian water tower now houses Dongta Coffee, permeating the park with its delightful aroma. Staff shops, gears, and sculptures of women workers in the hemp mill serve as reminders of the industrial legacy.

大运河1986文创园
GRAND CANAL 1986 CREATIVE PARK

园区入口处的晚峰书屋，经营中国古建筑榫卯积木，用中国榫卯记忆的传承来开发创新性益智产品；走入园区腹地，高大的红门布满金色大门钉，深藏着杭城首家沉浸式体验的古风短视频实景拍摄基地——大月传媒。在这里，农耕研学与麻纺回忆齐飞，缤纷文创与运河绿道共色。

The Wanfeng Bookstore at the park's entrance sells ancient Chinese mortise and tenon building blocks, developing educational products that honor the rich heritage of Chinese joinery. When I step deeper into the park, a towering red gate adorned with golden nails conceals Dayue Media, the first immersive ancient short video shooting base in Hangzhou. Here, agricultural study coexists harmoniously with the memories of fiber making, while vibrant cultural industries synchronize with the canal greenway.

文创园里还有一块特别可爱的遛娃基地——草莓君主题农场，让我一下子变成了小朋友。这片占地 108 亩的农场，是浙江绿鹰农业科技有限公司的大本营，以空中培育的方式种植"五色草莓""彩虹西瓜"等，形成一个集科普、采摘、研学、休闲等多功能为一体的农文旅草莓主题园区。在第 18 届中国（济南）草莓文化旅游节暨首届亚洲草莓产业研讨会上，这里选送的"越心"品种草莓在全国精品草莓擂台赛中荣获金奖。

There is also a particularly lovely place for kids in the Creative Park—the Strawberry Theme Farm, which takes me back to my childhood at a sudden as well. The farm spanning 108 mu of land is the main base of Zhejiang Green Eagle Agricultural Science and Technology Co., Ltd. Here, they employ aeiral cultivation to grow "five-color strawberries" and "rainbow watermelons," creating a strawberry-themed park that integrates science popularization, picking, research, leisure and other functions at one. At the 18th China (Jinan) Strawberry Cultural Tourism Festival and the 1st Asian Strawberry Industry Symposium the "Yuexin" variety of strawberries selected here won the gold medal in the National Strawberry Competition.

我亲眼见证，这里的草莓长在半空，没有其他地方草莓大棚里弯腰采摘、沾染泥土的困扰，草莓品相完美得像玩具，可见品控之严格。

I witnessed the strawberries growing mid-air in this very place. Here, troubles that people bend over to pick strawberries and that strawberries are stained with mud in conventional greenhouses do not have. The strawberries appear flawless, almost resembling perfectly crafted toys, a testament to the strict quality control measures in place.

东湖北路大桥
Donghu North Road Bridge

从 1986 文创园继续向东，微风春日，双桥村油菜花黄，如云似锦；运河两岸农舍田畴，如诗如画。

　　村里一路漫步，新农居有些颇有设计感，院子里苗壮生长的花草让人看了眼馋。双桥村在 20 世纪 70 年代是全国农业学大寨老先进、1978 年全国科学大会获奖集体，1979 年大队团支部获评新长征突击队红旗、"全国新长征突击队标兵"称号。为了纪念这段曾经的辉煌，村里建了农耕文化展示馆，展示曾经使用过的老法农耕工具与耕作方式。

Continuing further east from the Grand Canal 1986 Creative Park, on a gentle spring day with a light breeze, one encounters the breathtaking sight of golden rapeseed flowers in Shuangqiao Village blanketing the landscape like billowing clouds. On both sides of the canal, farmhouses and fields paint a picturesque scene, which adds to the beauty of the surroundings.

As I walked through the village, I couldn't help but notice the beautifully designed new rural residences, each adorned with vibrant flowers and flourishing plants in their yards. Shuangqiao Village holds a significant historical status as an model of advanced agriculture, particularly during the 1970s when it was recognized for "learning from Dazhai in agriculture." In 1978, the village's achievements were acknowledged at the National Science Conference, while in 1979, the Youth League Branch of the Brigade was honored with the prestigious Red Flag of the New Long March Commando, earning them the title of "National New Long March Commando Model." To commemorate this glorious period, the village has constructed a farming culture exhibition hall, showcasing the old farming tools and methods that were once used.

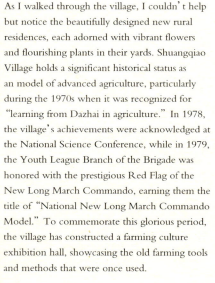

现在的双桥村，农业经济以生态甲鱼为主，是全国一村一品生态养殖示范村，也是中华鳖国家养殖标准制定者。而甲鱼于双桥，已不止于土特产，而是经创意提升转换为文旅物产。2023 年，围绕"甲鱼家族"文化设计的"双桥甲鱼"文化和旅游 IP 入选杭州市文化和旅游 IP 第二批培育名单。村里建起了有趣的甲鱼科普体验馆，展示着关于甲鱼的知识与文化。

Currently, Shuangqiao Village has become a national demonstration village for ecological breeding, with a focus on the cultivation of ecological soft-shelled turtles. It proudly carries the distinction of being a "one village, one product" ecological breeding model and has played a pivotal role in establishing national breeding standards for Chinese soft-shelled turtles. The turtles of Shuangqiao have transitioned from being a local product to a cultural tourism attraction through innovative promotion efforts. In 2023, the "Shuangqiao Turtle" culture and tourism intellectual property (IP), centered around the "Turtle Family" culture, was included in the second batch of cultivated IP projects under Hangzhou cultural and tourism. This recognition highlights the cultural and tourism potential associated with the "Shuangqiao Turtle" concept. To enhance the experience, an engaging Soft-Shelled Turtle Science Popularization Experience Hall has been established in the village.

甲鱼科普馆的北面，一路之隔，低平旷野，青苗白鹭，那是"爷爷的水稻田"，是青少年研学基地，也是杭州第一家"功能水稻"试验示范点。"爷爷的水稻田"项目，由中国作物学会特用作物专业委员会会长曾松亭博士于 2020 年发起，"爷爷"即为袁隆平爷爷。该项目让青少年走进水稻田，体验秧苗之趣，感悟"汗滴禾下土"的辛劳。

我期待秋天能再来双桥，欣赏金黄稻浪应和着运河的粼粼波光，在慧日寺悠扬的钟声里随风翻滚的景象。

To the north of the Soft-Shelled Turtle Science Popularization Experience Hall lies an expanse of green crops and white egrets known as "Grandpa's Paddy Field." Separated by a pathway, this area serves as a youth agricultural study base and the first experimental demonstration site for "functional rice" in Hangzhou. The "Grandpa's Paddy Field" project was initiated by Dr. Zeng Songting (President of the Special Crops Professional Committee of the Crop Science Society of China) in 2020, pays tribute to the esteemed Grandpa Yuan Longping. The project aims to provide young people with the opportunity to immerse themselves in paddy fields, allowing them to experience the joy of seedlings and gain an appreciation for the arduous work of "sweat dripping to the soil underneath the plant."

Anticipating a return to Shuangqiao in autumn, one can look forward to witnessing the golden waves of wheat swaying in the breeze and the shimmering canal waters. Against this tranquil setting, the melodious bells of Huiri Temple resonate, creating a symphony that truly captures the essence of the village.

杭州临平"爷爷的水稻田"
研学基地

在开辟研学基地之外，双桥村还推出"春有油菜、夏有插秧、秋有稻旅、冬有甲鱼游园"的双桥四时游玩计划，带动旅游产品经济，让更多村民实现在家门口就业、创业。

In addition to the agricultural study base, Shuangqiao Village has implemented a comprehensive four-season tour plan, offering visitors a diverse range of experiences throughout the year, including "rapeseed in spring, transplanting rice in summer, rice paddy trek in autumn, and turtles prancing in the garden water in winter." By showcasing the unique beauty and activities associated with each season, this tour plan helps to drive the tourism product economy in the village. Moreover, such a tourism initiative creates employment and entrepreneurship opportunities for more villagers, allowing them to engage in economic activities within their own community.

爷爷的水稻田

Grandpa's Paddy Field

by Yuan Longping

袁隆平

双桥村再向东，是以千亩荷塘闻名的新宇村。这里曾经是养殖甲鱼、黑鱼的示范村，但环境污染严重。在产业升级中，新宇村主动将养殖产业转型升级为"藕鳖套养""稻鳖共生"等新模式，为共同富裕进行了有益的探索。夏日的新宇村可是小红书上的"网红村"，千亩荷塘引来无数"打卡"拍照的网红与游客；同时，因荷塘产出的水果莲子在盒马等电商平台热销，顺势造就了村里平均年龄 70 岁、近百人规模的"奶奶工坊"，她们参与莲子脱粒的简单工作，销售旺季可获得每人每月 3000 元左右的收入。不仅如此，奶奶们通过莲子脱粒工作重新走入社会，为养老生活增添了一抹格外的亮色。

To the east of Shuangqiao Village is Xinyu Village, renowned for its a thousand mu of lotus ponds. Previously, it served to breed soft-shelled turtles and snakeheads, but the area suffered from significant environmental pollution. However, in a proactive effort towards industrial upgrading, Xinyu Village optimized and improved its aquaculture industry, embracing innovative practices such as "lotus root and soft-shelled turtle inter-planting" and "rice and soft-shelled turtle symbiosis." This endeavor has proven to be a fruitful exploration towards achieving common prosperity. During summer, Xinyu Village has become an Internet-famous destination on platforms like Xiaohongshu. The large lotus ponds attract countless online influencers and tourists who eagerly take a perfect snap. Simultaneously, the fruit and lotus seeds harvested from the lotus ponds have gained significant popularity on e-commerce platforms like Freshippo. This success has led to the creation of a "Grandma Workshop," comprising nearly 100 members with an average age of 70. These grandmothers actively participate in the simple yet important task of threshing lotus seeds, earning approximately 3,000 yuan per person per month during the peak sales season. Through this newfound opportunity, these grandmothers have reintegrated into society, adding vibrancy to their golden years.

新宇村千亩荷塘
Thousand-mu Lotus Pond in Xinyu Village

LISTING OF TRAVELING ROUTES

游踪小列

你怎么到临平？

高铁乘坐至临平南站，或者自驾，这些当然是最直接的。

如果是远道而来，在萧山国际机场、杭州东站、杭州城站或者杭州西站，换乘地铁就可以到达临平。

How to get to Linping?

Opting for the high-speed rail to Linping South Station, or driving oneself, certainly is the most straightforward way.

Should you arrive in Xiaoshan International Airport, Hangzhou East Railway Station, Hangzhou City Railway Station, or Hangzhou West Railway Station, Linping may be accessible via subway.

不同人群的不同玩法

★ 银发人群

< 一日玩法 >

 临平公园爬山 ⟶ 新天地文创园闲逛

⟶ 临平文化艺术长廊、戏曲艺术交流中心游玩并听曲

< 两日玩法 >

超山及江楠糕版艺术馆参观 ⟶ 塘栖古镇游赏

⟶ 古镇住宿 ⟶ 丁山湖段塘超小径漫步

⟶ 丁山湖农家乐用餐

⟶ 丁山河村百匠工坊参与传统食品制作

★ 情侣玩法

周末或节假日从杭州武林门乘坐运河水上巴士到塘栖古镇并游玩

⟶ 塘超小径漫步 ⟶ 塘栖村环湖卡丁车体验 ⟶

临平公园爬山 ⟶ 艺尚小镇闲逛购物 ⟶ 临平大剧院看演出

★ 遛娃人群

< 晴天玩法 >

临平公园爬山 ⟶ 东湖公园露营 ⟶ 新天地文创园晚餐

🍓草莓君农场草莓采摘 ⟶ 大运河 1986 文创园参观 ⟶ 东明路绿道漫步

玉架山考古遗址公园体验互动考古 ⟶ "爷爷的水稻田" 学农

杭州跑步中心运动 ⟶ 天都公园休闲漫步

< 雨天玩法 >

中国江南水乡文化博物馆参观 ⟶ 临平文化艺术长廊智慧图书馆阅读并听曲

临平大剧院欣赏演出 ⟶ 临平体育中心观看比赛 ⟶ 算力小镇地卫二航空航天科普馆参观

塘栖古镇漫步 ⟶ 法根食品体验馆参加体验课程

★ "特种兵" 玩法

塘栖古镇游赏 ⟶ 大运河绿道暴走 ⟶ 运河五杭景区徒步

⟶ 大运河 1986 文创园 "打卡" ✅ ⟶ 新宇村千亩荷塘留影

★ Silver-haired people

< One-day entertainment >

Climbing in Linping Park —→ Strolling along Xintiandi Cultural and Creative Park —→ Touring and Listening to Traditional Opera in Linping Culture and Art Corridor and Opera and Art Exchange Center

< Two-day entertainment >

Visiting Chaoshan Mountain and Jiangnan Cake and Pastry Mold Art Museum —→ Touring Tangxi Ancient Town and staying overnight —→ Rambling on Tangchao Trail of Dingshan Lake section —→ Dining at Dingshan Lake farmhouse —→ Joining in producing traditional food at Baijiang Workshop in Dingshanhe Village

★ People with kids

< During sunny days >

· Climbing in Linping Park —→ Camping at Donghu Park —→ Dinner at Xintiandi Cultural and Creative Park

· Strawberry Picking in Strawberry Theme Farm —→ Visiting the Grand Canal 1986 Creative Park —→ Walking on Dongming Road Greenway

· Experiencing interactive archaeology in the Yujia Mountain Archaeological Site Park —→ Farming at the Grandpa's Paddy Field

· Taking exercises at Hangzhou Running Center —→ Strolling in Tiandu Park

< During rainy days >

· Touring China Museum of Southern Water Town Culture —→ Reading and Listening to Traditional Opera in Smart Library in Linping Culture and Art Corridor

· Enjoying performance at the Linping Grand Theater —→ Watching competitions in Linping Sports Center —→ Visiting STAR.VISION Aerospace Science Museum in China Town of Computing Power

· Rambling in Tangxi Ancient Town —→ Participating in the experience course at Fagen Food Experience Hall

★ Entertainment for lovers

On weekends or holidays, taking the canal water bus from Wulin Gate to Tangxi Ancient Town for sightseeing —→ Strolling along Tangchao Trail —→ Experiencing go-kart around the lake in Tangxi Village —→ Climbing in Linping Park —→ Visiting and Shopping at E-Fashion Town —→ Watching performance at the Linping Grand Theater

★ Entertainment with hyper-efficient itinerary

Touring Tangxi Ancient Town —→ Long Walking on Grand Canal Greenway —→ Hiking in Canal Wuhang Scenic Spot —→ Ticking off the Grand Canal 1986 Creative Park —→ Taking Pictures at Thousand-mu Lotus Pond in Xinyu Village

最后，在这个视频都要短的年代，我们感谢所有耐心阅读这本书的人，就像我们要感谢那些愿意放弃私家车、使用公共交通的人。

In conclusion, in this era where short videos dominate, we should express our gratitude to those patient enough to read this book, like those prefer to use public transportation rather than their vehicle.

图书在版编目（ＣＩＰ）数据

古韵临平，时尚江南：汉英对照 / 王晓林绘；刘
冰婕文 . —— 杭州：浙江大学出版社 , 2023.10
ISBN 978-7-308-24247-9

Ⅰ . ①古… Ⅱ . ①王… ②刘… Ⅲ . ①区（城市）—概
况—杭州—画册 Ⅳ . ① K925.54-64

中国国家版本馆 CIP 数据核字 (2023) 第 187257 号

古韵临平，时尚江南
王晓林 / 绘　刘冰婕 / 文

责任编辑：周烨楠
责任校对：董齐琪　韦丽娟
责任印制：范洪法
封面设计：王晓林
出版发行：浙江大学出版社
　　　　　（杭州市天目山路 148 号　邮政编码 310007）
　　　　　（网址：http://www.zjupress.com）
排　　版：杭州地六文化创意有限公司
印　　刷：浙江海虹彩色印务有限公司
开　　本：787mm×1092mm　1/16
印　　张：7.25
字　　数：150 千
版 印 次：2023 年 10 月第 1 版　2023 年 10 月第 1 次印刷
书　　号：ISBN 978-7-308-24247-9
定　　价：98.00 元